# MILLENNIAL NASTIES

## ARIEL POWERS-SCHAUB

Encyclopocalypse Publications
www.encyclopocalypse.com

# CONTENTS

## PART ONE
The Nastiest Millennial Nasties

### THE NASTIEST OF THE NASTY
The Films That Built the Subgenre

# PART TWO
Original Slashers

## LIFE AFTER SCREAM
Slashers Get Nasty

# PART THREE
The Era of Remakes

## NASTI-FICATION FOR A NEW GENERATION
The Remake Surge

*For my nieces, Maddie and Allison. Dream as big as you want, girls.*

# FOREWORD

## BY ZOË ROSE SMITH

A few years ago, an email landed in my inbox with a pitch to Ghouls Magazine about an editorial piece focusing on the *SAW* franchise, and why these gory and torturous films deserved to be highlighted for their impact and importance within the history of the horror genre. I'd never personally thought of the *SAW* films as having much depth, but the pitch that came in made a quick and convincing argument that even though these films had a particular reputation for their use of gore, there was value within the narratives and even more so in the characters featured in these films. The article had already been written and was attached to the submission, so I wasted no time in reading it because my interest had really been piqued at that point. *'Make Your Choice: What Would Jigsaw Do?'* was an insightful, intelligent, and well-articulated piece of writing that unpacked the man behind the mask when it came to the now iconic horror character, Jigsaw. But the article didn't just look at this titular character, it carved through the flesh of others like Amanda Young, Detective Mark Hoffman, Doctor Lawrence Gordon, Doctor Logan Nelson and Jill Tuck. After reading the submission article, my immediate thoughts on the *SAW* franchise had been completely changed, and I was enamored by this rethinking about a film that hadn't received such an analytical critique before.

This was the first interaction I had with Ariel, and from the offset there was an energy and passion behind her love for the *SAW* films that I found to really encompass what being a horror fan is all about. Finding that passion for one particular film, or franchise or even sub-genre is what makes a fan of the work, but an even more dedicated and incredibly talented writer. At this point, Ariel had never been published anywhere before and was very open about this front—stating that she had a keen interest in breaking into the horror world with her writing, with a focus on found footage, *SAW*, folk horror and all things slashers. As the Editor-in-Chief at Ghouls Magazine, it's really important for me to be able to give budding writers the chance to be able to find their way into the world of horror journalism. For me, the journey was a long one that I spent many years cultivating and figuring out how to get my name out there, but over the years I realised it comes down to finding a passion in a certain area and really looking to own that area if you can.

My obsession came when I got into extreme cinema; anything that was disturbing, nasty and made most people want to never ever even read the Wikipedia page of the plot synopsis. For the past ten years I have been crafting my own voice within the horror world, constantly on a campaign to get more people to understand that extreme cinema is more than just taboo plotlines and over-excessive violence and gore, but instead provides catharsis, release and often explores the darker side of humanity. But my other passion in the horror world was to support other writers so they wouldn't have to spend as many strenuous years as I did trying to get work noticed by a magazine or outlet that I aspired to. The other aspect I noticed through those years was the lack of marginalised voices talking about horror films, yet the incessant want to hear more perspectives on horror from said voices. Which is why the goal with Ghouls Magazine was to accomplish both of those; give space to women and non-binary voices and support up-and-coming horror writers to break into the world and get their first piece of published work.

That's why when Ariel's email dropped into my inbox, I was instantly excited by the prospect of her joining the team because I could intrinsically sense just how passionate and dedicated she was to not only the horror genre, but to certain niches and even certain films like *SAW*. It didn't take long before Ariel began to show just how committed to horror she was; with such a wonderful way of delivering her thoughts on different topics and really expanding her voice across all things from slashers with *The Slumber Party Massacre* to found footage with *The Blair Witch Project* to torture porn with *Hostel.* It wasn't long before it became clear that Ariel was one of the most hard-working, genuine and enthusiastic people within the horror community, which is why I had to snap up the chance to ask her to become a senior contributor for us and to also get involved with press screeners, supporting other writers, extra content and co-hosting the podcast too. When you find someone who has an authentic love for horror, you just know that they are someone you want on your team, as part of your horror family, because it also meant I got to work with someone so amazing every day and help to support any projects that she would go on to do.

When Ariel told me she was writing a book about 00s horror films, with a focus on those categorised as torture porn and some of the nastier side of what came out of those years, I was so ecstatic. Whenever I think of films like *Hostel* or *Eden Lake* or *SAW* my mind immediately goes to Ariel because her knowledge on this sub-genre is so extensive, but also provides such a personal and analytical lens which seems difficult to do with films of this nature. I would always refer to Ariel as the Queen of torture porn and 00s nasty horror films, which is why reading through 'Millennial Nasties: Analyzing a Decade of Brutal Horror Film Violence' felt like such an honour and a somewhat depraved treat because not only does Ariel use her understanding and expertise of the sub-genres she explores within, but she also utilises her unique, personal and endearing voice throughout the book–a way of breathing life into her thorough deep dive through ten years of barbaric violence on screen and the horror films that defined the sub-genre. If you have been wanting a refreshing take on this often under-represented and misunderstood pocket of nihilism, torture and bleakness then prepare to get strapped into a Jigsaw contraption of sorts and allow Ariel to lead you through the darkness of treacherous traps, brutal and unflinching violence and gratuitous gore with an analytical lens that will open your mind (and body) to this important sub-genre of horror.

Zoë Rose Smith
July 2023

# MY COZY NEST OF FILTH

Thanks for picking up this book. This section is going to be a little personal, so if you want to get on with the horror, feel free to skip ahead.

My name's Ariel, not pronounced like the mermaid, more like how Sebastian the crab says it. I can honestly say I am a life-long horror fan, because I don't remember a time in my life before horror stories. They have always been my happy place. Born in 1987, horror of the 2000s was impactful to me, and these films have been involved in much of my life as a horror fan. In 2020 and 2021, I found myself writing about the *Saw* franchise to process my feelings about the COVID-19 pandemic. I was lucky enough to start writing for *Ghouls Magazine*, which led to other writing and speaking opportunities in the horror community. I am very grateful to *Ghouls Magazine* for the opportunities it has afforded me.

This book is a series of essays analyzing specific horror films in a specific time period (more on that in the next section). It includes some personal opinions and some of my own observations of the world around me. There aren't many books written yet that analyze this decade and subgenre, which is exciting, and a bit daunting. On a very personal note, this book has been inside of me for years, and I needed to get it out. I am so thankful that I got to.

This is not an academic text. I wanted to write my own analyses of these films, make my own points, not gather points made by others or slow down the reader with lots of citations. It's not a behind-the-scenes or a making-of text, either. Sometimes, production details are included when they were relevant to my analysis, but analysis remained my primary goal. It is not an exhaustive list of every film that could be explored, but rather the most important films to analyze for trends and themes in this time period.

This book should not be the final say on anything, and I hope more people feel welcome to the conversation about some of my favorite films after reading this book.

I was especially inspired by Alexandra West's books *Films of the New French Extremity: Visceral Horror and National Identity* (2016) and *The 1990s Teen Horror Cycle: Final Girls and a New Hollywood Formula* (2018), both published by McFarland & Company, and *House of Psychotic Women* by Kier-La Janisse (Fab Press, 2012).

Welcome to my cozy nest of filth.

Ariel Powers-Schaub
January 2024

# ANALYZING A DECADE OF BRUTAL HORROR FILM VIOLENCE

# FROM NOW ON, WE'RE CALLING
# THEM MILLENNIAL NASTIES

This book covers horror films from the early aughts, specifically the years 2000 through 2010. I know that's technically more than a decade, but I didn't want to leave out any films from these years. Many of the films covered have been called torture porn, and while that name was originally dismissive, it became the only classifier we have for this specific subgenre. I identify torture porn by these characteristics: a focus on over-the-top violence that's neither realistic nor cartoony. Rather, it's in an uncanny valley all its own; bleak stories; green and yellow lighting and filters giving the films a sickly look; a grittiness in the filmmaking that reflects a low budget or tries to emulate one; creative set pieces that result in death and pain, and English-language, primarily American and Australian. Torture porn has always been a misnomer: firstly, the films are not intended to be pornographic - to the contrary, they often got wide theatrical releases, and were seen by the masses, which was not the case for pornography. Secondly, torture is not always a factor in the films that get lumped in under this umbrella. No one has been able to agree on exactly what torture porn is supposed to mean. Is it derogatory, or proud? That depends on who's saying it.

Torture porn is different from another subgenre called New French Extremity, which this book does not analyze. I believe New French Extremity is its own cultural force with its own impact on the world, and it receives a relatively large amount of academic attention in horror analysis. I wanted to focus on films that have been often ignored. If you want to read an excellent book about New French Extremity, I recommend *Films of the New French Extremity: Visceral Horror and National Identity* (Alex West, 2016, McFarland & Company). Torture porn is also different from extreme cinema, which is a broad term that generalizes dozens of different films across the world and history. Because extreme cinema can be so broad, there may be overlap with torture porn, but again, many extreme films have been subject of abundant analysis. If you want to learn more about extreme cinema, seek out the works of Zoë Rose Smith.

This book is not only about torture porn. There are horror films of the same era that meet some of the torture porn criteria, but are different enough that they are hard to categorize. Original slasher franchises and remakes of classic horror films were popular during this time, and to keep horror audiences engaged, these films made use of some torture porn staples. One can also count on certain dialogue and jokes in movies of this time. There was an edginess to the writing, in many cases, trying to offend and push buttons. In reaction to some of the toned-down language in the 1990s, horror in the 2000s wanted to shock audiences. After all, if you offend everyone, no single group can boycott you.

And of course, many films at this time were influenced, either consciously or subconsciously, by the September 11th, 2001, terrorist attacks on the United States (which I will refer to as 9/11). Most of the academic writing about torture porn and similar films has been analyzing the impact of 9/11. America's sense of security from the 1990s was shattered. Suddenly, Americans were fearful of The Other, The Outsider. Bigotry made a huge comeback, though it never really left. And

American attitudes became both very sad and angry, stuck in an "us vs. them" mentality. This book is not focused on 9/11, but it is mentioned when relevant to the analysis. Horror films always reflect the world around them, and these films were born from global trauma. Throughout the subgenre, you can see fear of systems failing, that our walls won't hold us, and we need to fend for ourselves (however, American patriotism is always a safety net). There is plenty of military and police propaganda, and those organizations in the films are almost always heroes, not like the bumbling cops often portrayed in a slasher film. A phrase we heard often in America at the time was "the only thing that can stop a bad guy with a gun is a good guy with a gun," and it follows that Millennial Nasties are very pro-weapon. These films are often full of characters we don't like, so we can root for them to die. The TV news at the time was so graphic, Millennial Nasties had to increase the on-screen violence to keep audiences interested.

And now, I offer the film community a new term to use when referring to these kinds of horror movies of this era (torture porn and adjacent English language films of the 2000s). Let's call them Millennial Nasties.

**Defining Terms**

Speaking of terms, there are a few terms used in this book that horror fans might know but let me define them up front so we are all working with the same information.

A few terms refer to subgenres of horror or common horror characters. **Slashers** are a horror subgenre in which the story tends to be formulaic, and there is a killer, usually human, hunting and killing a group of friends one by one. Slashers almost always feature a **Final Girl,** a female character who survives the film, and usually the audience can pick her out early on. Dr. Carol Clover explained in her 1992 book *Men, Women, and Chain Saws*, there is often a Final Girl character that survives because she didn't give into the same vices of her friends, such as drinking and sex (pages 35-42). Final Girls in the Millennial Nasty era often wore white tank tops, dresses, or t-shirts, signaling their purity. **Folk horror** is another subgenre, but it's harder to explain than the formulaic slasher. Folk horror films often have an "us versus them" component, with out-of-towners running afoul of locals, and there is often a focus on the land, such as woods or fields. A common character in folk horror is the **harbinger**, who is a local, usually elderly, who wants the youngsters not to go to the area they are looking for. While the harbinger is roundly dismissed as a kook, he always ends up being correct. Another subgenre mentioned in this book is the **home invasion**. It's as straightforward as it sounds - a horror film in which the horror comes from someone coming to hurt the characters in their domestic space. It's straightforward, but open-ended and flexible, because the only limit is the horror people can inflict on one another.

An important term which inspired my choice of words is **Video Nasties**. While hardcore horror fans, especially fans from the United Kingdom, may be familiar with this term, many horror fans around the world are not. It refers to a list of films that were censored and banned in the UK, especially during the 1980s. I won't spend too much time on this topic - there are many books and articles written about Video Nasties, if you want to learn more - but know that when I refer to a Video Nasty, it means a movie that was controversial enough to be banned at some point.

### Prerequisite viewing

You do not have to have seen every film in this book to read the essays, though I warn you, the essays are full of spoilers. However, if I can suggest watching one film before reading, let it be Tobe Hooper's 1974 classic *The Texas Chain Saw Massacre*. That may come as a surprising recommendation, since it's not a

Millennial Nasty. It is, in fact, one of the original Video Nasties, and it has influenced horror ever since it hit drive-in theater screens. It is referenced throughout this book, as its influences impact the analysis of Millennial Nasties. Three characters are mentioned by name throughout this book, and I will credit them here:

- Sally Hardesty: the final girl, played by Marilyn Burns
- Pam: Sally's best friend, played by Teri McMinn
- Leatherface: the chainsaw-wielding killer, played by Gunnar Hansen

If you have seen the movies analyzed in this book, even better. Something unique about many of these films is how many versions exist of some of them. The 2000s were the height of the DVD era, and studios realized they could sell special features, unrated additions, director's cuts, and so on, with very little extra cost to them, and audiences would buy several versions of the same movie. When streaming was added to the mix, different versions ended up on different streaming services. While this was an interesting realization while writing this book, I also realized that it could add to some confusion. When I watched a specific version of a film for analysis, I noted it. In many cases, I have seen several versions of many of these movies, and they merge in my head as the basis for my analysis. If you watch a different version of the movie than I did, you may find new points to analyze.

Alright, enough set up. Let's get to the meat.

# PART ONE

THE NASTIEST MILLENNIAL NASTIES

# THE NASTIEST OF THE NASTY

## THE FILMS THAT BUILT THE SUBGENRE

In this first section of *Millennial Nasties*, we examine the unique films of this decade that were hard to categorize. They may have elements of other subgenres but didn't quite fit into any perfectly. Many of the films in this chapter have been called torture porn, either with disdain or with love. The trends set by these films early in the decade, especially the *Saw* films, would impact the Millennial Nasty films later in the decade. Aesthetic choices like grimy settings and green and yellow lighting, to dialogue choices that shock the viewer, to bleak themes and never exactly happy endings.

These films will take you on vacation, keep you trapped at home, subject you to the worst families you can imagine, and isolate you. They take you from intimate one-on-one settings to global conspiracies, and the darkness that lurks in the corners in between.

Dig into the guts and sift through the mud with me.

# MAKE YOUR CHOICE
## THE SAW FRANCHISE

Saw (2004), Saw II (2005), Saw III (2006), Saw IV (2007), Saw V (2008), Saw VI (2009), Saw VII/Saw 3D/Saw The Final Chapter (2010)

*Saw* is one of the first films mentioned when people talk about torture porn. Especially if they are saying something negative. A phrase I have personally heard many times when meeting another horror fan: "I like horror, but I don't really go for that torture porn stuff, like *Saw* or *Hostel*." For better and for worse, the *Saw* films are inextricably linked with the idea of torture porn. The first feature film was released in 2004, and every year after that through 2010. It's impossible to talk about this era of film without talking about the *Saw* franchise and how influential it was. If the era was full of gritty, nasty, violent, gory, grainy films, the *Saw* series was the trunk from which those nasty branches grew. Every *Saw* film was in dialogue with the rest of the genre, reacting to and influencing other films throughout the decade. As each *Saw* film ramped up the blood and guts, so did the other Millennial Nasties. This franchise is responsible for influencing the looks and atmospheres of other Millennial Nasties. The *Saw* franchise connects to every other film in this book, through cast and crew (see the Six Degrees of SAW-pera-tion chart at the end of this book). There are creative connections to other films in this book, as several filmmakers worked on the *Saw* films and other nasty films. The *Saw* films are the most important films in the Millennial Nasty subgenre.

Millennial Nasties are mostly from the United States, often exploring American fears, and that's interesting because Saw was created by two Australian men. (Australia is the other part of the world that offers many films to the Millennial Nasty subgenre.) James Wan and Leigh Whannell were students at the Royal Melbourne Institute of Technology when they made a short film called *Saw* (2003). Their short was successful, and the first feature-length *Saw* film played at Sundance Film Festival in 2004 and had a theatrical release from Lionsgate by Halloween that year. After the success of the first film, a sequel was greenlit immediately. Wan and Whannell lived the film student's dream and used their short film as a launch pad. They have both gone on to have extremely successful careers in the film industry, and *Saw* is the film that launched them. They co-wrote *Dead Silence* (2007) and *Insidious* (2010) (both directed by Wan), and they have both branched off on their own.

Throughout the *Saw* franchise, each film tackles multiple themes, and offers just as much plot and character development as it does blood and guts. The films in the *Saw* franchise all have similar setups, and a formula that gets more strongly entrenched as the decade progresses. The main villain (or anti-hero, depending on who you ask), is a man named John Kramer, a successful engineer and entrepreneur. After he suffers some personal tragedies, he begins trapping and testing victims of his choice, and makes them confront their own will to live. The press calls him Jigsaw because he always takes a piece of skin, shaped like a puzzle piece, as a trophy when his victims die. It was possible to keep strong plot threads in each film because of creative consistency. Members of the cast and crew worked on multiple movies, most notably Tobin Bell, the actor who played John Kramer/Jigsaw.

The themes explored in the franchise that are the most consistent throughout all have to do with family and loyalty. Jigsaw is particularly interested in fatherhood, and what it means to be a good father. The films in the franchise also offer an exploration of systems meant to help people, specifically the police and medical care. Some of the police officers portrayed in the franchise are genuinely trying to help victims and solve crimes. But several cops, especially the ones with central plot points, are crooked and cruel. The *Saw* films show the kind of tragedy and abuse of power can cause. When it comes to the American medical system, *Saw* has a lot to say in almost every film. John's wife, Jill (Betsy Russell), runs a free clinic and helps people suffering from drug addiction who can't get care elsewhere. John and Jill fight about her work, and he insists she can't help people this way, that his methods are better for making people appreciate life. Jill is doing selfless work in the community, and her husband doesn't support her. There is also a takedown of the medical insurance system in the sixth film, which will be discussed in more detail later in this chapter. The franchise does not get every criticism right – for example, mental illness and addiction are often portrayed as moral failings, rather than medical conditions. But that reflects American society at the time. One more strong theme throughout the franchise is revenge, and how seeking revenge can help or hurt you, and if revenge equals justice. While Jigsaw can convince himself his grudges are worthwhile, he discourages revenge in his followers. Whether or not you agree with it, the killer always has a motive, and just as John Kramer always said, "make your choice," the films allow you to decide who to side with.

It's best to watch the *Saw* films closely together, to follow the plot threads and twists. Each film has at least two related plots running side-by-side, though it's not always obvious how they connect until the last act. Often there is one plot following the victims in the traps, and another following the police as they try to catch Jigsaw. In later films, after the cast has expanded, other characters get their own plot threads, too. The plot is what kept the die-hard fans coming back for more. Audiences could find blood and guts in many films at the time. What made *Saw* special was the viewers' investment in the characters and how their stories would conclude. The *Saw* films strike a perfect balance of executing the formula to make money and giving the audience more each time to keep them coming back. But the first film can stand on its own as a horror classic, and the franchise and subgenre it launched had gigantic shoes to fill (with severed feet).

### *Saw* (2004)

"I want to play a game."

The first film in the franchise has the most straightforward premise: two men, apparently strangers, wake up in a disgusting bathroom, chained to the pipes, and there is a dead man face down on the floor between them. They find cassette tapes with instructions and certain rules to follow in order to survive. Neither man knows who would have trapped them or why, but they realize this must be the active serial criminal Jigsaw. While he never directly kills his victims, he is responsible for their deaths, when they don't pass his tests and die in his traps. Meanwhile, the police are trying to find these men, and exposition is shared through flashbacks of police investigating Jigsaw's other crimes. The cover art for the film is iconic as the story itself - one rotting foot, unattached to any person. Directed by Wan and Whannell, they expanded upon their original short film. Horror fans will never forget the feeling they got the first time they saw the twist ending of this film.

While there are some gory and bleak scenes, *Saw* does not fit the definition of torture porn. Because it was created by film students with other influences, early in the decade, it wasn't trying to be torture porn, or anything but a high-quality, low-budget horror film. The term torture porn didn't exist yet and *Saw* became responsible for many of the trends that followed it. Most likely, Wan and Whannell's influences had little to do with trends that came later. *Saw* certainly looks like a Millennial Nasty, with gritty and grimy sets and green lighting. Like the earliest slashers, it didn't know it was setting up a template for other horror films to follow. Much like the phenomenon that occurred with *The Texas Chain Saw Massacre* (Dir. Hooper, 1974), people remember *Saw* being more violent and gruesome than it is. Most of the torture and violence is implied, or kept partially hidden, most likely due to budget constraints of the debut filmmakers. Part of *Saw*'s signature look is the frantic editing, sometimes giving the film a feeling similar to a music video. The editing style trend happened accidentally, because the filmmakers didn't have the time or the budget to shoot enough takes of all the scenes they needed and decided to make up for it in the editing. That style of editing became a hallmark of the decade and torture porn genre, seen in many other Millennial Nasties in this book. Most of the film's impact came from the rush at the end of the film as the twist is revealed and explained, set against Charlie Clouser's iconic score. The song "Hello Zepp" would be used throughout the franchise to highlight the gut punch at the end of each film.

There were many elements that were independently scary but disconnected. Jigsaw's voice on the tapes, and the way he trapped his victims, were frightening elements used for furthering the plot in *Saw*. But Jigsaw also has a puppet that rides a tricycle, named Billy the Puppet, with a white face and a little bowtie, who rides into crime scenes and often moves his mouth along with the speech on the tapes. The puppet itself is creepy, but doesn't seem to fit with the rest of Jigsaw's plan. Similarly, when victims are kidnapped, the kidnapper is wearing a disturbing mask, with a realistic-looking pig face and long black hair. This first film doesn't offer any reason why that mask was chosen. But these independently frightening elements offer a disorienting and uncanny type of fear that makes us feel unsettled and unreal in an otherwise normal setting. It works better than anyone could have imagined. It feels as if Wan and Whannell were worried they wouldn't make another film, so they added in everything they could think of that they wanted to try. Later in the franchise, meaning is added to these elements, but the filmmakers had no idea that would be the case when they made the first film.

The main theme explored in the first film is the will to live. Part of the reveal at the end of the film is that John Kramer was dying of inoperable cancer and was frustrated with people around him who seemed unappreciative of their lives. He decides to trap people and put them through tests, always starting his recorded instructions with "I want to play a game." He offers his victims terrible choices about things they can try to do to survive or die in his trap. His thinly veiled anger at the world is masked by the motivation he says aloud. In truth, he wants to kill others, because he is frustrated that his life is being taken from him. The film focuses on two victims: Dr. Gordon, played by Cary Elwes, who ignores his family and plans to cheat on his wife, and Adam, played by Leigh Whannell himself, who is an angry person who gets paid to take pictures of others' private lives. With Jigsaw's focus on Dr. Gordon, this is the first we see of Jigsaw punishing fathers, which will continue throughout the franchise.

The film uses misdirection to make the audience think a different character is Jigsaw, but truly, we spend very little time with the person who becomes the focal point of the franchise. However, another important character is introduced. Amanda Young, played by Shawnee Smith, is more important than we realize when we see her in this first film. She is one of Jigsaw's victims who actually escapes her trap, which allows Jigsaw to deliver his iconic line: "Congratulations, you're alive. Most people are so ungrateful to be alive. But not you. Not anymore." Amanda becomes a follower of Jigsaw (which is revealed in the twist at the end of the second film), and has a tragic arc with a heartbreaking end, which could be the only outcome when someone follows a person like Jigsaw.

### *Saw II* (2005)

"What do you think the cure for cancer is?"

After the success of the first film, the second film came out of the gate just as boldly. Once again, there are two plot threads to follow. The police are hunting Jigsaw especially vigorously because he has taken a detective's son, named Daniel (Erik Knudsen). We are introduced to the aggressive detective, Eric Matthews (Donnie Wahlberg). Daniel wakes up with several strangers in an abandoned, dilapidated house. The strangers are all criminals of some kind, and slowly, they realize they have all been framed by Matthews at one point or another. They have to find the antidote for the poison in the air before it kills them. They are confronted by a series of traps along the way, which test their ability to follow directions. The audience thinks the twist comes early, when we see Amanda from the first film awaken in the house, but the film saves a few twists for the end, including that Amanda is working with Jigsaw.

Directed by Darren Lynn Bousman, this is the film in the franchise that set the formula that the others would follow. It set the template of starting with a group of characters who are killed one by one in traps that get more and more intense and ending with a twist. It feels tonally different from the first film. The focus is on a larger group of characters, many who are not as likable as Adam and Dr. Gordon were in the first film. There is less time for character development, and more time is spent on the gory deaths caused by the traps. It's also the first time the audience spends time with Jigsaw and learns more about his motivations and leave the audience eager to learn more in future films. After a cancer diagnosis and an unsuccessful suicide attempt, he decided to dedicate this life to testing the survival instinct in others. Jigsaw spends time talking with Detective Matthews, who is getting angrier and angrier, demanding his son back. Jigsaw says if Matthews just listens, his son will be safe. It turns out that Matthews is watching a tape of the strangers navigating the house, and his son has already been saved. Daniel is knocked out and locked in a nearby safe with an oxygen tank. This introduced us to the way Jigsaw follows his own rules, even if he doesn't always tell the whole truth.

A theme closely explored in *Saw II* is the impact of aggression on the people around you. Eric Matthews is not a good father or person - he yells at his teenage son for doing typical teenage things, and he has a history of framing and abusing those he arrested to close his cases. He's Jigsaw's actual test subject, not the people in the house. Jigsaw challenges him to listen, talk and listen calmly, and if he can do it, he will be given answers. Instead, Matthews gets frustrated and beats Jigsaw nearly to death. His explosive temper doesn't serve him well as a cop or a father, and it ultimately leads to him failing Jigsaw's test. His actions as a character feed the themes of the franchise exploring bad fathers, crooked cops, and playing by Jigsaw's twisted rules. Matthews ends the film trapped in the same bathroom from the first film, and Amanda locks him inside, with a strongly stated "game over" as she shuts the door.

*Saw II* continued what would become a pattern of ending on a twist and a character saying, "game over." By the end of the second film, the audience knew what they were in for. Future sequels were greenlit just as quickly and soon the tagline became true: "If it's Halloween, it must be *Saw*."

### *Saw III* (2006)

> "The rules of the game have been made
>   very clear."

The story is intimate and straightforward, like the first film. John is dying, and Amanda will do anything to keep him alive. They kidnap a surgeon, Dr. Lynn Denlon (Bahar Soomekh), and Amanda threatens to kill her if she can't save John. Dr. Denlon is forced to perform brain surgery with a power drill and whatever tools are nearby. Meanwhile, there is a seemingly unconnected man, Jeff (Angus Macfadyen), going through a series of traps by himself. After Jeff's young son was killed by a drunk driver, Jeff became isolated and spiteful, neglecting his young daughter. He is forced to judge a handful of people related to the legal case of his son's death and faced with the choice to kill them or let them live.

As in the first film, multiple people are being tested, but we aren't aware of all of them throughout the film. Jeff's test is the only one explicitly explained right away, but even then, not everything is revealed until the end. It is believable that Jigsaw would trap and test Jeff for being a bad father, based on the last two films. Jeff's final test is being faced with his wife, Dr. Denlon, and it's a surprising reveal that they were connected the whole time. The other person being tested, without her knowledge, is Amanda. Jigsaw wanted to see if Amanda could follow his rules, but it was a secret test, which is not usually Jigsaw's mode of operation. Maybe because she had passed a test before, he felt she was ready for the next level, a secret test. Whatever his reasoning, Amanda fails the test, and she dies, which Jigsaw knew was a possibility.

Amanda's arc is tragic. She starts to spiral and use drugs after she was framed by Detective Matthews, and she uses Jill's health clinic for services, which is where she meets John. She attaches herself to John and follows him with blind loyalty. This loyalty leads to her death, and Jigsaw was willing to let that happen, despite her devotion to him. He was not as devoted to her. Later films reveal more about Amanda's past and how her path overlaps with John's, but her death at the end of the third film just shows us a devoted follower dying because of her leader. Amanda's death is tragic, because she never got the appreciation she deserved, and Jigsaw was willing to throw her away.

Themes of family, loyalty, and revenge are prevalent throughout this film. Amanda is loyal to Jigsaw, but that only serves him, not herself. Jeff and Lynn end up being more loyal to each other than they realized, and after being tested, you can tell they want to be a functioning family again. But Jeff's desire for revenge ultimately leads to his and Lynn's deaths, proving Jigsaw's point that revenge is a bad motivator.

Bousman returns to direct again but *Saw III* feels more like the first film than Bousman's *Saw II*, and that's because Wan and Whannell were involved in the writing. This is the last film in which the original creators are directly involved, though they have producer credits throughout the series. There are fewer characters than in the second film, and we get to spend more time with them, which is reminiscent of the first film. But there are plenty of nasty set pieces, similar to the second film, including the Angel Trap, which rips out a ribcage, and The Rack, which twists a body's limbs until the person dies.

It could easily be the last film in the franchise, because Jigsaw and Amanda both die, and the ending feels final. The emotional stakes are high, and the payoff is worth it. But you can't kill *Saw*.

### *Saw IV* (2007)

"I promise my work will continue."

With Bousman directing again, *Saw IV* is a bold film. It answers questions and resolves plot points from previous films, and makes the viewer ask new questions and opens new plot threads. No film in the franchise had done that yet, each previous film feeling like it could be the end. The fourth film is the first time the series has to explore what it means for Jigsaw to be dead. Bell is still back, playing John Kramer in flashbacks, so it doesn't feel much different to the viewer. But throughout the film, the audience doesn't know who is setting the traps. The idea is introduced that Jigsaw might have more followers than just Amanda. At the end of the film, the big reveal (with "Hello Zepp" playing in the background, of course), is that a police officer, Detective Hoffman (Costas Mandylor), has been working with Jigsaw for years. He sets the traps throughout the fourth film, at the same time framing a colleague, Officer Rigg (Lyriq Bent). The two major plot lines running through the film are Rigg's going through traps set for him, and the police trying to figure out who is setting the traps.

The victims in the fourth film aren't like the victims we have met in previous films. Previously, Jigsaw wanted dads to be better to their kids, and families to stay together and love each other. He picked angry people who had a chance of being good. The victims in the fourth film feel like they are getting meaner punishments, sometimes for terrible crimes, sometimes for being faced with tough choices. If the viewer approaches this film thinking the victims were chosen by Jigsaw, it makes Jigsaw seem wildly inconsistent. But if Hoffman is the one choosing the victims, they start to make more sense. Hoffman is a police officer, and his sense of right and wrong is driven by his law-and-order frame of reference. He picks a sex worker, since he probably had to butt heads with sex workers trying to work around the law to make a living. He also chooses to punish a woman in an abusive relationship, and she has to kill her terrible husband to survive. Punishing survivors of domestic abuse does not seem like something Jigsaw would do, but a cop tired of going on those calls, saying "why not just leave him?" might. He also chooses a rapist, which I think Jigsaw would have agreed to. The rapist recorded his crimes to watch later, and the audience sees a little of one tape when Rigg has to watch it. Thankfully, the assault is not on screen for long. This is the only film in the franchise (so far) with any sexual violence, and it is not used for titillation. Rigg, himself, is being tested by encountering all these traps with others in them because Hoffman doesn't like his style of policing. Hoffman thinks Rigg is too impulsive and reactive. He's punished for rushing through doors to save other people, though it might endanger himself. Hoffman is planning for Rigg to die, and let him take the fall for the crimes, so Hoffman can mentally set aside justifying a good enough reason to test Rigg.

The theme of family is explored again, though this time, with more tragedy. A flashback shows Jill suffer a heartbreaking miscarriage after an accident at her clinic, in which someone was trying to steal drugs. John losing his son made him even angrier and added another layer of motivation to his crimes. He wanted to be a father so badly, and was robbed of that chance, so his desire to punish bad fathers makes some twisted sense. Loyalty is explored as well. Hoffman was working for John, but John seemed to know Hoffman would let him down, and the film ends with a tape of Jigsaw telling Hoffman that "his work would continue." Jigsaw values loyalty above all else, and he sensed Hoffman was being disloyal. It made the audience wonder how would that affect Hoffman in future films?

### Saw V (2008)

"Jigsaw doesn't make mistakes."

While this is David Hackl's directorial debut and his only directorial experience in the franchise, he worked in production on other *Saw* films and Millennial Nasties. Half the film follows a group of five people in a similar setup to *Saw II*. They are trapped together, going through tests and dying one by one, while trying to figure out how they are all connected. Eventually, they realize that they all played a role in a predatory development project. One of them burned a building down, killing eight people, another covered it up in the news, another one said the fire happened for a different reason, and so on. Because they each played a relatively small role, and didn't know about the bigger picture, their individual actions lead to the deaths of eight people. After most of the trapped victims have died, two survivors realize they all could have survived if they worked together. But their selfishness held them back. They were able to work together when they didn't know they were, to hurt others, but unable to work together to save each other, when it was pointed out to them. The other half of the film follows the dirty cop Hoffman, who is now being pursued by FBI Agent Strahm (Scott Patterson). The FBI is close to catching Hoffman, and there are several tense scenes where it seems like they may be catching on to him, but he keeps slipping away. Agent Strahm puts the pieces together, but Hoffman kills him before he can tell any of his colleagues, and Hoffman is off the hook for now.

*Saw V* reveals how Jigsaw and Hoffman came to be accomplices. The audience learns through flashbacks that Hoffman killed his sister's ex-partner, Seth (Joris Jarsky), after Seth murdered Hoffman's sister. Hoffman frames Jigsaw for the killing, but of course, Kramer knows he didn't do it. Jigsaw hunts down Hoffman and threatens to kill him or offers him the alternative of working together. Hoffman was always a more reluctant partner to Jigsaw than Amanda was. Amanda had been searching for guidance and someone to care for, and care for her. Hoffman never wanted anything but to avenge his sister's murder, and feels he has to work with Jigsaw or be arrested for his crime. Hoffman likes to do things his own way, whereas Amanda always wanted to please Jigsaw.

The main theme explored in this film has to do with the test of the strangers. If they had shared knowledge and worked together for the common good, they could have all survived and helped each other. But when they acted out of selfishness, everyone suffered. That ties into Hoffman acting selfishly by killing a person and framing another for the murder, and John trying to help by taking him under his wing.

*Saw V* did well at the box office but was not reviewed well. Audiences went to see it based on the *Saw* name, but they didn't love the story, which hurt the success of the next film.

### *Saw VI* (2009)

"Do you like how brutality feels?"

The director, Kevin Gruetert, had worked on previous *Saw* films, and was fond of the franchise, and you can feel it in the movie he made. It was co-written by Marcus Dunstan, who went on to direct other Millennial Nasties. *Saw VI* offers social commentary that hits hard and personally. The test subject is William Easton (Peter Outerbridge) who runs an American medical insurance company. He is portrayed as a miserly, evil villain who only cares about making money, not about saving lives. Meanwhile, the film follows Hoffman as the FBI is tracking him down, and Jill, who has been instructed by her late husband to kill Hoffman if she can. Both plots running simultaneously offer an exciting mix of gore, suspense, mystery, and all the things we have come to expect from the *Saw* franchise at this point.

Jigsaw set up a handful of tests for Jill to execute after his death, one of them Easton. John had a grudge against him because John tried to use insurance to cover an experimental

18

cancer treatment and was denied. John is taking out a personal grudge against one person who represents an entire system. While it makes for a great film, it shows cracks in John's logic. He wasn't always the measured, moral judge of character he wanted others to believe he was. It's cathartic to watch the insurance company get taken through Jigsaw's ringer, especially if you have ever had trouble paying for medical care in America. Easton is asked to choose between his coworkers who to save and who to kill, and they are presented the way his insurance company might frame them: old or young, healthy or unhealthy, family or no family. When Easton is faced with actual people, it's harder to apply his money-saving formula for who lives and who dies. The insurance company is compared in stark contrast to Jill's free clinic she runs to help her community. The *Saw* franchise has a clear stance on access to medical care, and the film offers an accurate examination of medical insurance through the Saw formula.

In addition to the exploration of medical care, family and loyalty are themes once again. Even though Jill wholeheartedly disagrees with John's crimes, she executes his last request of her, out of true love for him. Easton is also faced with the impact his decisions have had on families accessing care, and how his decisions in his own test affect his family. Combining societal commentary with killer games feels like what audiences want from a *Saw* film. Of course, the end delivers an excellent twist, one that I think is hard to see coming. The reception was favorable, but sadly, it made much less at the box office than the films that came before it. Likely in part due to the lackluster response to the fifth film, and also because it was up against a wide theatrical release of *Paranormal Activity* (Dir. Oren Peli, 2007) that Halloween. Because *Saw VI* made less money, the studio decided to wrap up all the loose ends in the next movie and be done with the franchise.

## *Saw VII* (2010)

"Game over."

*Saw VII* is the last *Saw* film of the decade, but definitely not the last in the franchise. In 2010, the Millennial Nasty era was winding down, and the *Saw* franchise felt like it needed to wrap things up, even though more films were initially planned. *Saw VII* suffered from production issues, from directorial changes, script rewrites, and trying to cram too much plot into one last movie to answer all the viewers' questions. The whole ends up feeling like less than the sum of its parts.

Though Gruetert returns to the director's chair, it doesn't feel much like a *Saw* film. It feels rushed. It still has the traps and the morality tale, this time with a liar being punished for profiting off his lies. There is a self-help guru touring and making a living off of the book he wrote after surviving one of Jigsaw's traps. However, it's all a lie. He was never tested by Jigsaw. John Kramer found out about this, before his death, and put a plan in motion to test this person and make him face the traps he said he survived. But the character is hard to sympathize with, because he is awful to his wife, and the rushed story makes what could have been an interesting plot feel thin. However, the gore and the traps deliver. The other half of the film is a game of cat-and-mouse between Jill and Hoffman. One of the victims from the first film, Dr. Gordon, returns, and if you think that's the twist, the actual twist is that Gordon was working with Jigsaw all along! Dr. Gordon was instructed to keep an eye on Jill, and if anything happened to her, to kill her killer. Eventually Hoffman does kill Jill, with the reverse bear trap originally intended for Amanda. The women who were dedicated to Jigsaw had fates so entwined, all because they felt loyalty to the wrong man. Jill's death feels rushed, which is sad, because she became a central character, and the audience didn't get much time to sit with her tragic end. Dr. Gordon kills

Hoffman, finally putting a stop to him after more than half the franchise. Then the planned franchise simply ends.

The themes in this film are weak, because the focus was on wrapping up plot points. Loyalty to Jigsaw is explored, but not as deeply as it was in other films. The opening death in this film is the only death in the franchise that doesn't tie back to other characters or story threads in some way, it just seemed like an excuse to get more 3D gore into the film. There is an interesting death scene in which white supremacists are being tortured and killed. That makes sense in the plot and also within the morality of Jigsaw. What makes that scene interesting is that there are other Millennial Nasties in which white people try to solve racism by killing individual racist people. Keep an eye out for that later in the book.

There is very little Jigsaw in this film, in person or in spirit. This film relies more heavily on CGI than the other films, and it was shot in 3D. There was a short period of time when 3D movies were popular, but they did not look good on high-definition televisions years later. In any case, the journey from the original film - two men trapped in a bathroom, their will to be live being tested - to the seventh - Jigsaw's wife running from Jigsaw's copycat while one of the original victims returns in a twist - is quite the journey.

"I promise, my work will continue."

Thankfully, fans didn't have to end on that note, and there were additional sequels. It's my personal hope to see many more *Saw* franchise entries in my lifetime. But the first seven films, following Jigsaw, Jill, and their life together, tell a story that defined the decade. Every single film in the *Saw* franchise during this time serves as a backbone of the era. With a new movie out each year, each movie strengthened the latest trends and gave other films something to compete with. Villains were compared to Jigsaw and the *Saw* films were used as a scale by which to judge the gore in other films.

Even as the franchise changed hands and grew into something new, it never stopped being gritty, gory, nasty, and focused on punishment as justice.

After all that work, you would think Jigsaw and his followers need a vacation...

# BETTER STAY PUT

## VACATIONS GONE WRONG

HOSTEL (2005) AND HOSTEL 2 (2007), TURISTAS (2006),
CABIN FEVER (2002), AND WOLF CREEK (2005)

During the Millennial Nasty decade, American characters were often portrayed as afraid of the world. In America's reality, it was becoming clear that people in other countries didn't necessarily trust us, as global citizens watched America's involvement in war. That feeling of mistrust led to a trend in filmmaking where some vacationers - usually young and beautiful tourists - went off to an unfamiliar area and didn't make it home. Tourists, especially white tourists, in these movies are hunted and killed for their physical and national characteristics. This wasn't strictly an American fear, however. An excellent example from Australia, *Wolf Creek*, explored similar themes. *Cabin Fever* fits in this chapter, as well, although the fear is domestic and biological, as campers and a small town are picked off by a disease. However, the fear of the disease leads to person-on-person violence and represents the nastiness that can happen when Americans fear for their safety and try to protect themselves. In each of these films, vacationers are hoping to rely on the kindness of strangers for help, and they are let down in the worst ways.

## AMERICANS ON VACATIONS ABROAD

### HOSTEL (2005) AND HOSTEL 2 (2007), TURISTAS (2006)

#### *Hostel* (2005)

"I'm an American, I have rights!"

Together with the *Saw* franchise, *Hostel* and *Hostel 2* are usually the first films mentioned when people talk about the era of Millennial Nasties. In fact, *Hostel* was the first film to be called torture porn in writing, in a 2006 article by David Edelstein in *New York Magazine*. The *Hostel* films also ushered in the trend of films about vacations gone wrong, especially highlighting American fears about traveling abroad. As I wrote in my review of *Hostel* in *Ghouls Magazine* (2021):

> Eli Roth's *Hostel* (2005) follows the fates of three young men on a European backpacking trip. Paxton (or Pax) (Jay Hernandez), Josh (Derek Richardson), and Oli (Eythor Gudjonsson) are "boys' night out" personified, in pursuit of drugs and sex in Amsterdam. They meet a local named Alex, who tells them that the best girls can be found in hostels in Bratislava, Slovakia. He says that these women will be particularly interested in American men. Taking the advice, they head to Bratislava. … As guests of the hostel start to go missing, Pax, Josh and Oli slowly uncover the truth. Alex and the women from the hostel are working together to sell American tourists to Elite Hunting, a secretive group which accepts money in exchange for the chance to torture and kill a person."

— POWERS-SCHAUB, 2021

While the Elite Hunting group captures and sells people from all over the world, Americans are the most expensive, and it's implied that's because people want to kill Americans the most. The year 2005 was a time when much of the world was at the very least wary of Americans, and at most, hated us.

Eli Roth was inspired to write the story of *Hostel* when he heard a rumor about a website on which an individual could pay to murder another person. He wanted to draw comparisons between the exploitation that happens when people vacation places like Amsterdam, and the disregard for the humanity of sex workers. He drew a line from that kind of vacation ramping up into a murder vacation (Condit 2006).

*Hostel* is supposed to be making fun of Americans, high-lighting the ways we can move about the world in boorish ways, anticipating everyone to meet our needs. And *Hostel* could have made this point, but it just misses. By focusing on the male characters who are victimized, and keeping the story tightly centered on their experience, *Hostel* does not take time to comment on human trafficking and exploitation or American exceptionalism. In fact, the film has the opposite effect, making people angrier at Americans. Slovakian officials decried the film and said it was offensive to depict their culture in such a way (BBC News 2006).

What places *Hostel* so firmly in its era is the behavior of the characters, the attitude toward consent, and the bigoted and offensive humor trying to be edgy. The beginning of the movie is about getting to know the men on vacation, likely to inspire sympathy in the audience. However, the men are so off-putting, the sympathy is hard to muster. They use homophobic slurs, objectify women, start fights and yell about being American. From my review on *Ghouls Magazine* (2021):

> There are a lot of naked women, several sex scenes, and a leering camera. It's impossible for me to look past how this film treats women. While we don't see very many women in danger,

most of the women fill one of two roles: sex object, or evil monster. One could say this movie is about taking shots at objectification and misogyny, and women ultimately having the power. After all, objectified women use their looks to their advantage. Our three male leads would never think to worry for their own safety, especially in regards to beautiful women. But then those beautiful women sell them to a torture club. However, that fact is not enough to counteract the sexism we see and hear from the characters and the camera. Many misogynistic comments are made, such as from Paxton as they are leaving a brothel, when he jokes that he hopes bestiality is legal in Amsterdam because "that girl is a fuckin' hog." Later, the camera forces the audience to take part in the objectification of women when it pans up and down on the body of one of the hostel staff. It's not that we see a character look her up and down, the audience is forced to do so. Hostel is not a movie about misogyny, it is misogynistic.

While society still has a lot of work to do understanding the issue of consent, we have come a long way in 2005. At the time, consent was not often a topic acknowledged in media, unless lack of consent served the plot (such as in rape revenge films). But *Hostel*, perhaps accidentally, makes points about consent, albeit seemingly at random.

This movie's ideas about consent are inconsistent. Consent is acknowledged a few times, albeit crudely. For example, the guys meet a woman who is clearly stoned, and Paxton says, "We can't rail a girl that's in a coma. I think that's illegal, even in Amsterdam." At a later point, when the boys are on a train, a strange man touches Josh's thigh, and Josh reacts by jumping up and yelling at the stranger. While Josh's reaction is coming from a homophobic place, the movie (maybe accidentally) makes a point about consent. But then there are scenes where consent is completely ignored or outright dismissed. When the boys go to Alex's (Lubomír Bukový) apartment for the first time, they see a naked couple having sex. Oli excitedly sits near the couple and stares at them, which Alex encourages, because "they are so fucked up, they don't even know what planet they are on." A few minutes later, as Alex is encouraging the boys to go to Bratislava to find women to sleep with, he remarks, "you just take them." Hostel was released in 2005, and culturally we have a much better understanding of consent now than we did then. But I think even in 2005, Alex's comment would have been a red flag. For a movie that's all about bodily autonomy, regarding either sex or torture, it really doesn't make a clear point about consent.

— POWERS-SCHAUB, 2021

The focus on men's experiences in *Hostel* is a unique one. Men are crying and begging for their lives in this film. That did not fit the macho portrayal of masculinity that was so prevalent in this era. It also subverts a trope that relies on purity being a saving grace in horror films. Drawing on our knowledge of the Final Girl, the audience may think Josh will be the lone survivor, because he resists the temptations of Amsterdam the most, though he is not perfect. But in fact, Pax is the Final Boy, who has been trying to influence Josh the whole time. Josh ending his night early is what gets him caught before Pax. *Hostel* succeeds in flipping a horror trope on its head to surprise audiences with a Final Boy who loves sex and partying. That was surprising and refreshing at the time. While the majority of the film is young men trying to pay for sex and drink as much alcohol as they can, the last act certainly earns the Millennial Nasty title with its violent torture scenes. Audiences were waiting for this part of the story since the opening of the film, which shows someone whistling and casually cleaning up blood in one of the torture rooms. The last act is a great horror film in and of itself, with impressive fight scenes and all the disgusting gore a horror fan could want. The cinematography and editing are done with loving attention to detail, and it seems like the greatest amount of attention as paid to the last act. The torture chairs have become iconic, and anyone who has seen this film can recall particular tortures, such as the slashing of Josh's Achilles tendons and what fans call the "eyegasm scene," when Pax trims Kana's (Jennifer Lim) dangling eye.

The setting of the torture factory has the familiar texture and look of the gritty, grimy Millennial Nasties. It's dark and damp, there are rusty tools laid out, and just looking at it makes you feel dirty. There is an affectionate nod to *The Texas Chain Saw Massacre* (1974) when one torturer drops a chainsaw on his leg, just like Leatherface did. But unlike when Leatherface cuts his leg slightly, the chainsaw goes all the way through the torturer's leg and cuts it right off. There is interesting attention paid to the female characters who are luring the men, Natalya (Barbara Nedeljakova) and Svetlana (Jana Kaderabkova). The actresses are beautiful, and it would be a tall task to make them look any less. But their beauty is particularly played up in the first part of the movie, when they are on the job, acquiring men for Elite Hunting. Their shiny hair, perfect makeup, and revealing clothing are like a work uniform. Pax runs into them when they are off the clock, so to speak, in a townie bar after successfully trapping Oli and Josh. The filmmakers chose to make the women look more natural - little to no makeup, hair clean but undone, jeans and casual t-shirts. It gives the feeling of the ruse slowly falling apart as Pax gets into deeper trouble.

The closest *Hostel* comes to suggesting Americans would be better off with more knowledge of the world is when Pax tries to save himself by speaking German, which the torturer speaks. By pleading in German, he makes his torturer hesitate for a moment, but ultimately this strategy does not save Pax. The movie ends with the message that Americans should indeed be scared to travel to other places, where they will be hunted and killed for sport.

## *Hostel 2/Hostel: Part II* (2007)

> "Don't tell me what I can't afford, there is
>     nothing I can't afford."

*Hostel 2* (sometimes written as *Hostel: Part II*) was released two years later. It tells a similar story with female characters at the center, and it's a more successful film in every way. There is more character development, better dialogue, more tension, and an excellent balance between disturbing realism and violent disgust. The film follows the stories of both the victims and the killers, which offer a wider view of the whole world, and allow for deeper fear to take root. The film briefly shows people all over the world - different ages, races, and genders - bidding on the victims captured by Elite Hunting. They are on their personal laptops with their families around, or at work with an extra tab open on their desktop, casually bidding for the lives of others. That scene alone offers more existential fear than the entire first film. Not only does it show the truly global and insidious reach of Elite Hunting, but it shows the casual and cold cruelty of those looking to murder others. It also works as a better horror film because the horror starts much earlier. There is a creepy harvest festival, in which one character gets lured away, and dread sets in about what may happen to her. The kills in this film are more creative and messier than in the first film, and there is more to enjoy as a horror fan, from the disturbing story to the special effects.

*Hostel 2* makes its point, where the original missed the mark. The sequel shows the global scale of the human race's growing indifference to cruelty and makes a point about capitalism when the main character's money saves her. Around this time, the world, and particularly the United States, was still reeling from the news of torture in Abu Ghraib prison. In 2004, photos were released that showed American soldiers torturing prisoners in the name of the War on Terror. Through 2006, soldiers were legally held accountable for their war crimes and human rights violations, but the damage was already done, and the photos were truly horrifying. *Hostel 2* shows the casual cruelty of people all over the world, as the world was processing something even more monstrous, supposedly happening in the name of freedom. Audiences were getting desensitized to violence, and escapism and catharsis were sought (Hersh, 2004).

In this film, the two featured killers are wealthy, white, American men who want to take an indulgent murder vacation. Their names are Todd (Richard Burgi) and Stuart (Roger Bart), are motivated differently. Stuart wants to kill a woman who looks like his ex-wife, which is such a whiny, fragile reason to commit murder, and it feels, unfortunately, possible. Todd wants to give off a vibe that other people should fear him, and he compares it to knowing who the first guy in high school to have sex was. Their casual, breezy approach to murder as a bucket-list item and way to climb the ladder make up some of the scariest parts of the film. They discuss their approaches and strategy while on a jog, as if discussing an upcoming business project. They laugh and play with props at the torture factory. It's not even as if they see other people as worth less than themselves, and therefore within their rights to kill. In fact, they have completely dehumanized the people they are going to kill, in the most extreme form of objectification of women by men.

The interesting women in this film somewhat make up for the awful portrayal of women in the first film. The main character, Beth (Lauren German), comes from extreme wealth. That is to say, she has such an unimaginable amount of money; the number is never stated. It's left up to the audience to fill in the blank with whatever number makes us balk, and that works well in the story. It doesn't matter how much money she has, not really, just that she has plenty. She is the unfortunate soul who looks like Stuart's ex-wife, and she almost talks her way out of him, killing her. In the end, she buys her freedom from Elite Hunting, and becomes a killer herself by killing Stuart. In a cathartic and well-earned moment, she cuts off his genitals and feeds them to the dogs, letting him bleed to death.

Apart from Beth's wealth, the women in the film are capable and have agency. Whitney (Bijou Phillips) is coded as the sexy party girl and still treated with respect. She enjoys sex, and that mostly goes uncommented on. Lorna (Heather Matarazzo) is whimsical and quirky, in a realistic way. She doesn't care what others think, and while she isn't as assertive as her friends, she asserts herself in the world in the ways she wants to. It's notable that Beth is queer, but that's never made part of the plot or conflict in a way different from the non-queer characters. Beth is lured in by a woman named Axelle (Vera Jordanova) who works for Elite Hunting, lured by a beautiful woman like the men in the first film. It's no different from the way Lorna is pulled in by a man. In *Hostel 2*, one of the top people running Elite Hunting is an older woman. Whereas *Hostel* portrayed the evil as a very narrow subsection of humanity - sexy women lure you in, rich men kill you - *Hostel 2* shows the diversity in evil, which can be counted as progress in the Millennial Nasty era.

While *Hostel 2* is progressive in some ways, from social commentary to filmmaking choices, it still fits beautifully into the Millennial Nasty box. It relies on edgy humor, making jokes at the expense of others and not caring who it might offend. The violence in the film includes dogs eating a man, a kid getting shot, an attempted rape, and headless body being munched on by a cat at a kitchen table, and - most memorably - Lorna hung upside down, screaming, while she gets her throat cut and her killer washes herself in her blood. The Lorna killing brings to mind Pam's murder in *The Texas Chain Saw Massacre* (1974). In that film, Pam is hung on a meat hook, and the way it's filmed and acted, audiences would swear up and down they saw the hook go in. But they didn't; it's not shown. Lorna's death is similar. There is violence shown, but it's much more felt than shown. The scene focuses on her screaming and crying face, and on the reaction of the person bathing in her blood. That might be more effective than if they had shown her being mutilated in great detail, without the facial reactions.

*Hostel 2* updates the message of the first film: anyone can be dangerous, even people like you. (After all, don't Beth and Stuart have a lot in common?) However, the second part of the message is, if you have enough money, you can do anything. And what better way to frame an arrogance that was so culturally intrinsic to America at the time.

### *Turistas* (2006)

"I just wanna go home."

John Stockwell's *Turistas* follows a group of Americans and the dangers they face abroad, and it fits so perfectly into the Millennial Nasty camp. It's snugly nestled in time between *Hostel* and *Hostel 2,* released in 2006, with a budget similar to what *Hostel 2* would have. But it didn't have as much of a reach and didn't do as well domestically or globally. That means not as many people have seen *Turistas* as have seen the *Hostel* films, but it was playing with similar themes. It's not as violent. There are more scenes of people reacting to pain rather than what's causing the pain, and it relies on the implications of the subject matter to create its horror.

It follows a group on vacation in Brazil, tourists from America, England, Australia, and Sweden. All white, all English-speaking, though the Swedes talk to each other in Swedish. Their tour bus crashes and while waiting hours for the next bus, they find a bar in a secluded part of the beach and decide to party all night. It's quickly revealed to the audience that Brazilian locals are kidnapping tourists, especially "gringos," and stealing their organs to save the lives of Brazilians in need. Most of the film is either the tourists being led to their demise by a local who pretends to be on their side, Kiko (Agles

Steib), or being led away by the same local who decides to actually take their side.

Kiko is practicing his English and enjoys talking with the white tourists. He is secretly working for the doctor harvesting organs, who happens to be Kiko's uncle. But as Kiko gets to know the group of strangers and becomes torn about the right thing to do. He says something to the effect of, "I've never made friends with a gringo before. I have never really talked with one." He feels guilty and conflicted about passing them off to his uncle. Eventually, Kiko changes sides, and decides to help the tourists escape, which gets him shot and killed. The character of Kiko only exists to help the white tourists escape alive, and the fact that he is killed shows a disregard for him. The only local character the audience is supposed to have sympathy for only exists to serve the white characters, and once they are safe, Kiko is no longer needed. It's a racist and thoughtless use of a Brazilian man in this story.

Because the film takes place mostly outside, it doesn't fit the gritty look of other Millennial Nasties. The underwater cinematography is beautiful, and the gorgeous forest feels like the direct opposite of the torture factory in the *Hostel* films. The scenery serves the horror by reminding the audience how far away from home the tourists are. There are a few aspects of the film that fit the Nasty aesthetic. The tourists are robbed after they pass out at the beach party, and that gives the film an excuse to keep the sexy actors in swimsuits for the whole film. Some of the surgery scenes are a little dirtier and grittier than the rest of the film, taking place in a small makeshift operating room and happening with urgency, and there is some frenetic editing that brings *Saw* (2004) to mind during those scenes. Even the morally corrupt doctor has something in common with Jigsaw: he monologues through his torture and justifies his actions as a means to a desirable end. There are tense chase scenes and a few gory surgery scenes, but most of the horror comes from the idea that traveling outside your home country could end with your organs being removed.

The tourists, especially the American man, Alex (Josh Duhamel), act boorishly. Not only does Alex refuse to speak Portuguese, but he also doesn't realize it's a different language than Spanish. He says the bus driver should "go pick bananas or something," and refuses any piece of Brazilian culture he might enjoy, opting for a Coke rather than a local drink. But remember, acting like a crude American doesn't necessarily get a character killed in Millennial Nasties. Like Pax in *Hostel*, Alex survives *Turistas*, and instead of reevaluating his preconceptions, he decides he *was* right all along and acts like non-white, non-English-speaking countries are all as dangerous as he suspected. This film rewards the actions of a brash, brazen American.

Audiences didn't have to travel far to find things to fear. Some of it was right in our backyard...

## Americans Unsafe Domestically

### *Cabin Fever* (2002)

> "You two can fuckin' rot. Not me, no
> fuckin' way, not me!"

Released early in the decade, *Cabin Fever* is undeniably a force to be reckoned with as a Millennial Nasty. It's one of the bleakest and nastiest films in this book, and there was still most of the decade left to go. This is a vacation-gone-wrong story, but unlike the other films covered in this chapter, the horror is domestic rather than abroad. While Eli Roth and his co-writer Randy Pearlstein started the story in 1995 (Wixson 2010), it perfectly reflects the fear many Americans felt in their own country at the time. America is big enough that we can conjure fear of The Other right in our backyard. There has always been a fear of rural communities and what they get up to when city folk aren't around, and there are several examples of those stories in this book. *Cabin Fever* is different, though, because the fear is fueled by sickness.

The film follows five friends, college students who go off for a remote cabin-in-the-woods vacation, a setup familiar to many horror fans. They immediately begin partying, including drinking, drugs, sex, and even shooting a gun they found. Two of the guys, Jeff and Bert (played by Joey Kern and James DeBello) make a bet to only drink beer all weekend, which becomes relevant to the plot. A stranger comes out of the woods, visibility sick and coughing up blood. After that encounter, the friends start to get sick, too, and they need to find a way to get out of the woods and get help before they all die. The disease is a flesh-eating bacteria spread through the water, so it turns out that drinking only beer was a surprisingly good plan. Roth was inspired by an actual skin infection he experienced, during which he accidentally shaved off parts of his face (cinema.com date unknown). *Cabin Fever* is a love letter to horror films, with many nods and homages to the classics Roth grew up with. But it's also tonally bizarre. There are certain characters and scenes that don't add much to the narrative and don't fit what else is happening. For example, there is a memorable character named Dennis (Matthew Helms), a young boy who sits outside the general store who yells, "PANCAKES," does karate, and bites people. He could be removed, and not only would it not hurt the narrative, but the story would also make more sense.

There is nastiness in the gore and in the actions of the characters. The disease is introduced in the story via a dead dog that rips apart when his owner tries to move him. As Marcy (Cerina Vincent) is shaving her legs, after contracting the disease, her skin is peeling off. Paul (Rider Strong) falls into a reservoir with the diseased corpse of the sick man from earlier in the film and is completely drenched in the germs that make him sick. Karen's (Jordan Ladd) face is partially eaten away by a dog, and as she lays dying, Paul kills her by smashing her face over and over. During an entertaining but unnecessary scene, Paul tells a story of a break-in that occurred in his hometown, in which several employees of a bowling alley were brutally murdered. As he's telling the story, we see it acted out, which adds a little more nastiness to the film.

There is also behavioral nastiness, which rivals the gore and body horror. There is a racist joke that is meant to pay off later in the movie, but it wasn't funny in 2002, and it's not funny now. The students also casually use bigoted language that would be out of place in horror today. One of the most shocking scenes takes place with Karen and Paul in bed. Lifelong friends, Paul developed a crush on Karen and was trying to find a way to tell her how he feels. When Karen first becomes ill, she spends a lot of time dozing in bed. At one point, Paul gets in the bed with her, and starts touching her sexually without her consent. She doesn't even seem to be awake. The horrific part of this scene is meant to be that he's actually been touching and fingering an open wound on her leg, not her vagina. Which, yes, would be decidedly gross. But the true horror of the scene is that he's sexually assaulting her, taking advantage of a person who cannot consent. More recent conversations about this film acknowledge that, but in 2002, there was not widespread criticism of this scene.

If *Cabin Fever* was simply nasty, it may have gotten lost in the sea of Millennial Nasties to come later in the decade. But it's one of the bleakest, most nihilistic films of the time. The characters are all horrible - they are not nice to each other; they barely seem to be friends. They are thoughtless about the world around them, ungrateful to be in college, and completely selfish. Bert shoots a sick person instead of helping him because he fears for his own safety. He does nothing else to help; he doesn't even tell his friends about the event. When they start to get sick, they turn on one another quickly, and would rather leave their friends behind and protect themselves. When Paul is the only one left, the corrupt cops dump him in the woods, where he dies near the water. Paul never got a chance to explain that the town's water was contaminated. The film ends with showing how far that water will travel. There are kids unknowingly selling contaminated lemonade at the general store, and trucks shipping water to other cities. The implication is that this disease will spread far and wide. Over the end of the film plays a Bluegrass version of "Swing Low Sweet Chariot," providing a lively and upbeat tune about death. While most of the movies discussed in this book have survivors and a shred of hope, there is no hope to be found in *Cabin Fever*.

Because it was so early in the decade, the Millennial Nasty checklist had not been established yet, and *Cabin Fever* meets some of the criteria, but not others. It has red hues instead of gritty greens and yellows. The cops are evil and kill innocent people instead of being portrayed as heroes. But there is person-on-person violence, because where there is fear, violence is likely to follow. It subverts the Final Girl trope by killing Karen early, and eventually, subverts a lot of viewers' expectations by killing everyone. It's a gross film about mean people who hurt one another out of fear. It's definitely a Millennial Nasty.

NOT JUST AMERICA...

## *Wolf Creek* (2005)

"You never know where I might pop up."

Fear of The Other has never belonged to Americans alone. Tourists from around the world can fear their vacations. A quintessential vacation-gone-wrong film from this era is an Australian gem called *Wolf Creek* (2005). Greg McLean's *Wolf Creek* opens with a note that the story is "based on true events," and crime statistics about people going missing in Australia. The story is loosely based on real Australian serial killers who targeted tourists. *Wolf Creek* follows three young backpackers who are tricked, tortured, and killed by a serial killer named Mick (John Jarratt). It's a unique Millennial Nasty because it does not focus on American fears. The backpackers are two British women and one Australian man - no Americans involved.

Like many violence-focused films at this time, the plot is straightforward. The group of friends is comprised of Kristy (Kestie Morassi), Liz (Cassandra Magrath), and Ben (Nathan Phillips. The backpackers' car breaks down while they are exploring the site of a meteorite. Mick offers to fix it for them, and drugs and tortures them after earning their trust. The violence doesn't begin until almost an hour into the film, but then it never lets up. The first part of the film is spent getting to know the tourists, with a focus on the beautiful land they are exploring. Unlike the portrayal of Americans on vacation, such as in *Hostel* and *Turistas*, the *Wolf Creek* tourists are mostly respectful. They make some rude comments to locals who are harassing them, but otherwise seem to mind their own business and are interested in exploring the Outback. They are three loveable people; they are not caricatures of bad tourist behavior.

In the beginning of the film, when the backpackers are safe, the scenery is bright and dusty, like it would be hiking in the Outback. There are wide shots of beautiful scenery, all nature, no city. Once the violence begins, the aesthetic changes to the gritty green and yellow we have come to know and love in this era. The character of Mick changes from a friendly, jovial hick to a nasty, mean sadist. As he's planning to rape Kristy (which does not happen), he says to her, "I always use a rubber with you cunts, I don't know where you've been." This line, along with the pile of body parts Liz finds, tells the audience that Mick has been doing this for a while, and will continue to do it.

The photos and personal belongings of his previous victims demonstrate that he will torture and kill anyone who crosses his path, including children. There's a woman's dead body hanging up in the shed, headless, and Mick insinuates he was raping her corpse until he could lure new victims. Within minutes, Mick turns into one of the sickest characters imaginable.

*Wolf Creek* subverts the Final Girl trope by killing Liz. She is resourceful - she escapes her ties, shoots Mick in the neck (though he lives) and makes a plan to get her and her friends out. But she is the first to die. Rather, her spine is severed, and Mick calls her a "head on a stick," so even if she is still alive, it won't be for long and she can't run for help. This comes as a devastating shock. Kristy almost makes it. When she's running in daylight down the road, a la Sally Hardesty (Marilyn Burns) in *The Texas Chain Saw Massacre* (1974), the strength of the reference tells the audience Kristy will be fine. A lone woman escaping in daylight, horror fans know what that means. A driver even stops to pick her up. But we are shocked when bullets fly, and she and the unsuspecting driver are sniped by Mick. The women's bodies are never found. Ben escapes, and is picked up by strangers, relying on the kindness of good Samaritans, which is what got his friends killed after they offered help from Mick to fix their car. His life is ruined, not only due to the torture he endured, but because he is accused of hurting his friends. While his name is eventually cleared, their bodies are never found, and no one has any closure. That's a bleak ending, but there is some hope that because Ben escapes he can tell his story. Still, I think he will be hesitant to take any road trips.

## Stay Home, Fear Everyone

Horror has long been a genre that judges and punishes indiscretion, including having too much fun, so it follows that vacations would be punished in horror. The combination of global fears combined with audiences' bloodlust brings us vacations-gone-wrong horror stories. Everyone wants to feel safe, and if you have to venture out, you hope to rely on the kindness of others. But these films told us it was best to just stay home. Which brings us to the next chapter...

# LOCK YOUR DOORS
## HOME INVASION

### The Strangers (2008) and The Collector (2009)

Home invasion has existed as a horror subgenre for a long time, and with good reason. You might not believe in ghosts or demons, but there's always the possibility that another person could break into your home and hurt you. Sobering reality is what makes home invasion films so scary. Not unlike the national fear the United States after 9/11 - we were caught by surprise in our own home. Two Millennial Nasties that invaded our homes were *The Strangers* and *The Collector*.

### *The Strangers* (2008)

"Because you were home."

Bryan Bertino's *The Strangers* perfectly captures the anxiety and helpless feeling of many Americans after 9/11. It's a basic, stripped-down home invasion story. There aren't twists or surprises or even much exposition. It's two innocent people caught unaware, attacked for no reason.

The screenplay was loosely inspired by the Sharon Tate

murders and a series of break-ins in the writer/director's neighborhood as a child (Universal Studios, 2009, p. 3).

The film opens with a screen reading "inspired by true events" and violent crime statistics. It seems like it's meant to evoke feelings similar to Tobe Hooper's *The Texas Chain Saw Massacre* (1974), which has a similar introduction. Immediately, the film squashes any sense of hope or comfort, because the ending is shown first. We overhear an emergency call, and someone saying, "We found people," while the camera pans through an empty house and a bloody mess. It's no secret the characters are going to be hurt and possibly killed.

The movie has a unique feeling from the opening - it's quite sad and somber, with a man and a woman in formal clothing driving at night. They are completely silent, and the woman has tears on her cheeks. We learn that James (Scott Speedman) proposed to Kristen (Liv Tyler) at a friend's wedding, and her response was, "I'm just not ready yet." James had planned a beautiful evening of celebration at a remote family vacation home, complete with champagne, scattered rose petals, and a candlelit bath. The sadness of the couple against the thoughtful celebratory setting invokes sympathy and heartache. It's a far cry from the party atmosphere that opens many horror films, especially slasher films and films focused on couples. There is no drunk partying, loud upbeat music, or keg of beer.

The up-close-and-personal feeling is enhanced by intimate shots of Kirsten and James. Before the violence begins, the scenes are quiet and close. The only sound is some mellow country music from a record player. A slightly shaky camera and the private setting suggest the audience is watching something real unfold. It's an efficient and effective way to help the audience care about the characters quickly, because there is little exposition. It's never stated how long they have been together, whose wedding they were attending, or why they decided to go to this house together instead of their separate ways that night. A future road trip is briefly mentioned. It's unclear what they do for a living, or even if they are good people. But the audience knows just enough to feel sympathy for characters who don't deserve what is coming to them. After the 9/11 terrorist attacks, that's how many Americans were feeling, too.

Kristen and James make for an interesting representation of masculinity and femininity at the time. Aspects of their characterization would likely be considerably different if this film were made in the present time. For example, Kristen smokes cigarettes. In 2008, not only was smoking more common in films, but it was also more common in reality. As public knowledge increased about the health hazards of smoking, smoking became more exposed as a health hazard, filmmakers and production studios realized they could get more money by not showing cigarettes in their films. Smoking would potentially give your film a higher rating from the Motion Picture Association, which meant fewer kids could see your movie. Smoking would not be viewed as sympathetically now. Kristen's cigarettes are used as the McGuffin that gets her alone in the house. She runs out of cigarettes, so James takes a drive to get her some. If this film was made today, it's more likely medicine or food would have been used as the reason to go to the store. Smoking cigarettes would now be framed as a character flaw, not a reason to leave the house.

Though Kristen broke her boyfriend's heart, she is portrayed as caring and kind. She is sad about hurting her partner's feelings by refusing his marriage proposal, but she prioritized honesty, and was gentle about it. It positions the audience to feel more compassion towards James and Kristen. They are kind and affectionate to one another, at least until the horror starts. Emergencies will always push the boundaries of politeness. James acts like he believes Kristen at first, when he returns from his errand, and she says someone was in the house. He grabs a knife and searches the rooms one by one. Most likely, he was just doing this to appear heroic, because later he says to Kristen with frustration, "Nobody came in here," when he needs to go out by himself to get his cell phone from the car. He's framed as a masculine hero for part of the film, protective of Kristen, and trying to comfort her, even if he is patronizing her.

But later, the film changes its opinion of James. He finds his father's shotgun, and Kristen is relieved, but James admits he doesn't know how to shoot it or even load it, and that he had been lying about growing up hunting with his dad. Kristen seems disgusted by this, not only the lie, but that an American man in 2008 does not know how to use a gun. The audience is supposed to agree this is a character flaw. America has always had a fraught relationship with guns, to say the least. But at a time when the country felt threatened, guns became even more highly valued, and a sign of masculinity and stability. James is somewhat redeemed by what he says later. Kristen asks him, "Why are they doing this?" He replies, "Don't think about that, doesn't matter right now. We don't need a reason if they come through that door." Americans at the time were feeling strongly justified in retaliating with violence when they were under attack.

It's no accident that the film's killers are the direct opposite of the main couple–the audience knows nothing about them and feels nothing for them. There are three killers, one man and two women, and they are all masked. No personal details are revealed about them, and there is no discernible reason for their actions. The most famous line from the film is when Kristen asks the killers why they are doing this, to which they respond, "Because you were home." That was the American fear at the time - that we might be minding our own business and get killed for no reason. The film's killers prioritize torture. They could have murdered James and Kristen quickly, but instead they instigate a game of cat-and-mouse before tying them to chairs and stabbing them, somewhat anticlimactically. Before the stabbing, the killers unmask. Normally in a film, this would be a moment of clarity, but it does nothing for Kristen and James. There is no understanding, no moment of realization, which may feel worse than if they recognized their tormentors. They are stabbed and left for dead on the backdrop of a gorgeous remote wooded area. As the killers drive away, one tells another, "It will be easier next time." It's horrifying to hear that they plan to do this again, without any more motivation.

Kristen is almost dead, but alive enough to scream at the end of the film. It's Christianity that saves her, in another obvious sign of the time period. Young boys are going door-to-door, offering Christian pamphlets, and that's the only reason she is found before she dies. The final message of the film: you may have done nothing wrong, but if you want to save yourself, Christianity is the only way. At this time, there was a lot of hate for non-Christians in America. *The Strangers* delivers a not-so-subtle message that Christianity is our only hope in the face of those who want to torture and kill us.

The horror in *The Strangers* comes from the tension and the hopelessness. It's not all that violent, especially for the time period in which it was made. But every attempt to escape is thwarted. No neighbors are around. Their one friend who comes to help is accidentally shot by James. And it's all happening on a backdrop of rose petals, reminding us that even if they get out alive, they are returning to a sad situation. The film is a well-executed, bare-bones Millennial Nasty.

### *The Collector* (2009)

"He always takes one."

Written and directed by Marcus Dunstan, who has writing credits on several *Saw* films, and created near the end of the era, *The Collector* doesn't pull any punches when it comes to gore, disgust, and hopelessness. It was originally pitched as a *Saw* (2004) prequel, but the studio wanted to have it stand on its own (Miska, 2009). It's a unique twist on home invasion, because there are two invasions happening in the same house.

ARIEL POWERS-SCHAUB

The antagonist, known only as the Collector (Juan Fernández), has broken into the house of the Chase family to torture and kill them. Protagonist Arkin (Josh Stewart), on the other hand, broke in for unrelated reasons and wants to steal from a wealthy family to pay off a debt in desperation. Neither home invader knows the other will be there, and they suddenly become obstacles for one another. Pitting Arkin and the Collector against each other in a contained cat-and-mouse chase blurs the lines of who deserves to suffer, and who we are rooting for. The straightforward plot of the film highlights the economic insecurity and the fear of Americans' safety plans failing us at the time.

The structure and aesthetic of the film fits neatly into the Millennial Nasty box. Over-the-top visual effects are used to elicit disgust and push the audience to their limits. There is skin ripping, fingernails popping off, entrails flopping on the floor, and a nauseating moment with a needle in an ear. The house has been booby trapped by the Collector, and the traps are inno-vative and shocking to watch. The cinematography often focuses on the more complicated traps, and we see tracking shots showing every part of the Rube Goldberg-style killing machines. A respectful nod to the traps in the *Saw* films, they were an efficient way to deliver violence to the viewers who were looking for it. While the film has many moments of tension, and is suspenseful throughout, most of the horror is portrayed through the guts and gore. The music and sound design add to the sickening feeling for the viewer. The music is either nu-metal (popular in the 2000s) or melancholy, moody chords, depending on the scene. Throughout the scenes with the Collector, there are often screeching, screaming sounds in the background. It's not diegetic, it's meant to be part of the background experience heightening the tension of the movie. Sounds of human agony used as background noise is unique, and it works for a Millennial Nasty. In addition to the body horror, insects and arachnids are another central visual anchor for the film. The Collector himself works in pest extermination, but he shows care to the insects in the house, delicately placing a spider out a window before returning to his torture victim.

There is a striking juxtaposition between the two families in the film. Arkin and his ex-wife have a tense relationship, trying their best to care for their young daughter Cindy (Haley Pullos), but they are being chased by loan sharks. Arkin does contracting work on houses, which gives him opportunities to case the homes of people with more money, and later rob them. He steals from the rich not for a love of crime, but out of desperation. The year 2009 was during an era of economic recession in the U.S. and around the world, and many people who previously felt secure were suddenly in desperate financial situations. This reality makes Arkin a relatable and loveable audience stand-in.

In contrast, the Chase family is not only financially secure, but wealthy. Michael Chase (Michael Reilly Burke), the husband and father, is a jewelry broker. While there is some family tension with their teenage daughter, Jill (Madeline Zima), they otherwise seem like a nice, normal family, which happens to have a lot of money. In fact, they have an alarm system, so it's not as if they are naïve to the possibility of danger. The Chases can afford to pay several contractors to work on their house, to keep it safe and secure for the family. The fact that their safety measures don't save them highlights the insecurity Americans were feeling at the time about their safety.

Place the wealth and security of the Chases next to the stress and hardship of Arkin's family, and it's easy to root for Arkin, because so many viewers can relate to financial stress. As soon as the Collector becomes a factor, we are rooting for Arkin and the Chases. The Chases didn't do anything to deserve being tortured and killed, and the film gains a complicated layer by positioning the audience to feel sympathy for who they thought would be the bad guys. Arkin could have taken the gem he came to steal and bolted, or he could have just run off with nothing to save himself. Instead, he stays in the house and attempts to save the whole Chase family. This makes the audience feel good, because if we related to Arkin's financial hardship before, now we can feel like heroes. The audience was satisfied to see the wealthy family at the mercy of a working-class man.

Focused more on violence than sex, The Collector only has two sexual scenes, used to convey starkly different feelings. The first is Arkin meeting his criminal contact in a strip club, wherein there are brief shots of women pole dancing, and the audience is supposed to view Arkin as a beacon of righteousness in a den of sin. The second sexual scene is when the Collector is watching the teenage daughter Jill and her boyfriend Chad (Alex Feldman) start having sex in what they think is an empty house. This scene is meant to both titillate and disgust. As horror was wont to do at the time, the camera goes for titillation by focusing on Jill's breasts, though she is supposed to be a teenage girl. The disgust comes watching the Collector watch her - he licks his lips through his mask, evoking memories of Leatherface doing the same in The Texas Chain Saw Massacre (1974), and he's obviously enjoying sexual voyeurism before killing the teens. Overall, the focus of the movie is on non-sexual violence.

Though the film is named after him, we don't know much about the Collector. He is a masked, unknown figure - he could be anyone. All we know is that humans are lower than insects to him, and he wants to hurt and kill us. The Chase family die without ever understanding what was happening to them, which may be a universal fear, but was an especially American fear in this time. The tone of The Collector is "please save us from the bad people who want to hurt us," and it's topped with a layer of blood and guts, very fitting of the time period it reflected. But something unique about the film is that the police are not the heroes. A police officer shows up while Arkin and the Chase family are still trapped, and the Collector kills him. In many films during this time period, police and military personnel were usually portrayed as heroes, coming to save the day. This was the feeling in America after the terrorist attacks, and it could be seen as part of a propaganda campaign to get more people to enlist in the military. But in *The Collector*, the first police officer is killed trying to rescue the family. After Arkin gets the youngest daughter out of the house, police and medical personnel are there to help, but Arkin was the one who got them out. The film captures another feeling that was pervasive in this time period: you're on your own, and if you need something done, do it yourself.

## No Place Like Home

In both films, the acts of violence are committed by strangers with no motivation other than to torture, hurt, and kill. The torture takes different forms - psychological in *The Strangers* and physical in *The Collector*. Both show characters that, while flawed, seem realistic and haven't done anything to earn this treatment. They lock doors, try to call for help. They are at the mercy of the killers and things end badly. Home invasion films made more recently have been much more hopeful, and included resourceful characters who can fight and survive, especially women (such as Adam Wingard's *You're Next*, 2011, and Mike Flanagan's *Hush*, 2016). Marcus Dunstan directed a sequel to *The Collector*, called *The Collection*, in 2012. *The Collection* takes the action out of the home, but the Collector himself is just as menacing. A third film was planned, but unfortunately it may never materialize, after production issues. After *The Collection*, a new franchise began with a home invasion, when *The Purge* was released in 2013 (Dir. James DeMonaco). *The Purge* uses a home-invasion setting to deal with issues of class and socioeconomic status. In 2018, the sequel *The Strangers: Prey at Night* (Dir. Johannes Roberts) was released, and the same masked killers torture another family across an empty mobile home community. It's clear that home invasion films were moving away from the straightforward fear of having your door kicked in. The helpless feeling of the early 2000s is not as prevalent in current fears, even if we will always fear an intruder in our homes. And even if our homes aren't invaded, we may still have to watch out for...

# FUCKED UP FAMILIES

MAY (2002), HOUSE OF 1000 CORPSES (2003), THE
DEVIL'S REJECTS (2005), REPO! THE GENETIC OPERA
(2008), THE LOVED ONES (2009)

The danger has narrowed focus, from around the world, to our
own homes, to our own families, each setting harder to escape
than the last. It is deeply American to tout one's family values
and insinuate you would protect your loved ones at any cost. A
loyal family unit can protect one another while putting others in
danger, or just hurt one another because of their proximity.
Spending some horrifying time inside a family unit, and the
pain family members can inflict on each other, offers much for
the horror genre to explore. And the Millennial Nasty era did
not pass by this fertile ground. In a time when horror films were
disgusting and violent, that opened up many doors for horror
to smash through.

*May* **(2002)**

"If you can't find a friend, make one."

*May* (Dir. Lucky Mckee) is a gem from early in the decade that flew under the radar at the time, but in recent years, has been getting more of the attention it deserves. The titular character May (Angela Bettis) is a quirky, strange, and lonely young woman, but seems kind and interested in others. The film starts in her childhood, and it's clear she's had trouble making friends. Her mother (Merle Kennedy) gives her a homemade doll and says, "If you can't find a friend, make one." May has a lazy eye, which her mother encourages her to hide and tells her that other children won't want to be her friend if they see her condition. She has internalized this advice into her adulthood, shyly keeping to herself and becoming a loner. What was meant to be a kind of encouragement from her mother has made May into a lonely adult. Adult May doesn't seem to have any family connections or close friends, other than her flirtatious coworker Polly (Anna Faris), and a man she is interested in dating, Adam (Jeremy Sisto). She is on her own a lot, which is difficult for her, because all her approval comes from outside sources. She learned from her mother to view other people as their parts, often commenting on body parts of others, and looking for someone whose parts are all likable.

May's quirks range from harmless to violent. She works at an animal hospital so she can play in the blood and guts while helping animals at the same time. She enjoys telling stories about the grossest surgeries and giggles at the memories. When she brings Adam home on a date, she serves him macaroni and cheese with Gatorade to drink, and they sit at a makeshift table with mismatched furniture. She talks to her doll, makes more dolls, and makes her own clothes. On the macaroni-and-Gatorade date, Adam shows her a short film he made. He is undoubtedly trying to both impress her and disgust her, as he tried to do before by showing his collections of oddities and the weapons in his room. He wants May to be a little afraid of him, so he can keep the power in their relationship. The short film depicts a couple on a picnic, who start making out, and eventually are cannibalizing each other. May is turned on by this, and as she and Adam move to the bedroom, she bites his lip and draws blood, which scares him enough to end the date and leave. May can't understand why he would have shown her that tape if he wasn't interested in biting as a sexual kink. So far, she is quirky, but not dangerous.

Where May's behavior crosses the line is when she reacts violently to rejection. Her mother taught her to view people as parts, and her doll-making reinforced this idea. Therefore, that's how she views other human beings. When Adam rejects her because she is too weird, May gives up on trying to find a perfect match, and decides to make one, as her mother advised her all those years ago. The final act of the film follows May, cutting up her friends and acquaintances to make the perfect best friend for herself. She removes one of her own eyes and gives it to her creation, Amy, an anagram of her own name. She begs her new friend to see her, because all May wants is to be seen. The ending is surprisingly sad, after a darkly funny movie during which we are rooting for May. When she realizes her plan won't work, and she can't make a new friend after all, the movie ends on a beautiful and bleak note. The tone, visuals, and the unique story make *May* a Millennial Nasty to stand the test of time.

## ROB ZOMBIE'S FIREFLY FAMILY

### *House of 1000 Corpses* (2003) and *The Devil's Rejects* (2005)

> "One day he just got up and went pure
> devil on us all."

The Firefly family are icons of the Millennial Nasty era, created by Rob Zombie and featured in *House of 1000 Corpses* and *The*

*Devil's Rejects.* Though both films have overlapping characters and aesthetics, they provide experiences different enough that some fans enjoy one film but not the other. In the first film, the family is victimizing tourists, but in the second film, they become the victims.

*House of 1000 Corpses* follows a young friend group composed of two couples: Jerry and Denise (Chris Hardwick and Erin Daniels), and Bill and Mary (Rainn Wilson and Jennifer Jostyn) who are road-tripping across the United States visiting roadside attractions. Their plan is to write a book about America's unique roadside stops. This brings them to Captain Spaulding's (Sid Haig) Museum of Monsters and Madmen, where they learn the legend of the brutal serial killer Dr. Satan, and they go looking for local landmarks related to the legend. On the way, they blow a tire in pouring rain, and get a tow back to the Fireflies' house. From this point, the audience is still aligned with the young couples, but the Fireflies are the focus of the film.

In 2021, I wrote for *Ghouls Magazine:*

> Jerry and Bill, ignoring protests from Denise and Mary, take the group on a hunt for Dr. Satan's crime scene. On the way, they pick up a hitchhiker, a sexy and irreverent woman called Baby (Sheri Moon Zombie). Suddenly they blow a tire, or really, their tire is shot out by a man in a bear costume, R.J (Robert Allen Mukes). It's revealed that Baby and R.J. are brother and sister, members of the Firefly Family. The four roadtrippers go back to the Firefly home to wait for R.J. to fix the car, where they meet the other Fireflies, including Otis (Bill Moseley) who is angry and loud, Mother (Karen Black) who plays innocent, Tiny (Matthew McGrory) who seems like a gentle giant, and finally Grampa (Dennis Fimple), the blustering head of the household. Meanwhile, we see flashes of a news report that five local girls,

highschool cheerleaders, have gone missing. The tension at the Firefly house builds, through uncomfortable conversations and cringey stage performances. In a way, the Firefly family is "playing with their food," and torturing the group of friends before killing them.

The comparisons to *The Texas Chain Saw Massacre* (1974) are obvious. A group of young people wander where they shouldn't on a road trip, and a murderous family traps them to kill them one by one. However, *House of 1000 Corpses* feels incredibly unique, in a way that only Rob Zombie could execute. Pulling again from my 2021 review in *Ghouls Magazine*:

The plot is not what makes this movie special - it's the feeling and experience of watching. Captain Spaulding inviting the audience into his Museum of Monsters and Madmen is a strong opening to *House of 1000 Corpses* (2003). It feels like an extended music video, with cuts to unrelated shots that don't advance the plot, and to characters who do not become a part of the story. It's footage spliced together to enhance the feeling instead of the narrative. There are overexposed negative shots, and harsh expositions from broad daylight to the dark of night. The vignettes of the Firefly family are meant to remind us of the tapes made by the Manson Family cult. So much of what we see is unexplained, which is jarring in the best way. The Firefly house has tons of texture, and unsettling props everywhere. The visuals and the sound design are equally impressive. The varied soundtrack, the electric guitar, Baby's grating laugh, Otis yelling and ranting, and tolling bells make this a creepy listening experience. It's not surprising that Rob Zombie would have a handle on sound design. This is one of the only movies I can think of where the visuals are so impactful, you could watch it without the sound, and the sound is so thrilling, you could just listen without watching. You can almost feel what it would be like inside the house, to touch the dolls Baby has hung on the walls, or to smell the mushy food Grampa is licking off his plate and spitting out when he yells.

*House of 1000 Corpses* is a staple of the Millennial Nasty era, and also somehow apart from it, because Zombie started the film in an earlier era. Production wrapped in 2000, but the film had to go through many cuts to be considered suitable for audiences. And then 9/11 happened, and many horror films were significantly cut and/or delayed as the world reacted to the tragedy. This combination of events adds up to a film that was released into an era that was ready and waiting for violence and nihilism on screen, but created in an era where that was a fresh take on horror. That makes *House of 1000 Corpses* feel timeless, in a way some other films discussed in this book will not (Devine, date unknown).

In my 2021 review for *Ghouls Magazine*, I describe what puts this film snugly in its era:

> Rob Zombie used this movie as a conduit to talk to the audience, and to challenge us. Though this movie would later be called torture porn, there is no sexual violence. However, there are many close-up shots of faces and bodies of dead women, which, even if not explicitly sexualized, are very clearly on display more than men. And there is a lot of overlap in sexiness with horror imagery. For example, images of women stripping while also playing with toy skeletons. There are several shots where characters are talking directly to the camera, in a way that can make the audience feel exposed. In the opening, when Captain Spaulding is being robbed and not backing down, the last thing he says to the robbers is "and most of all, fuck you," and shoots a gun at the camera. This tells the audience that Zombie does not care about our boundaries, and we are in his world now. Later, when the danger is obvious and we are worried for our main characters, the local cops find one of the cheerleaders, dead and in the trunk of a car. She is naked, and

has the words "trick or treat" carved into her skin. As the camera lingers on her body, we hear Otis in a voiceover, saying over and over again, louder and louder "hope you like what you see!" The audience is forced to sit with the horrifying image, and question why we may, in fact, like what we see. Near the end of the film, as Denise and Jerry are dressed and bound for sacrifice, Otis speaks to Jerry, but looks directly into the camera and tells the viewer, "It's all true, the boogeyman is real and you found him." I hear this as Zombie claiming to be Hollywood's new boogeyman, a hopeful statement when this was filmed. This film means to push your boundaries and have you question your own comfort with what's on screen.

— POWERS-SCHAUB, 2021

*The Devil's Rejects* (2005) provides a different atmosphere, more action than horror, while still being a loving tribute to '70s grindhouse filmmaking. The Firefly family is the focus this time. They are being chased by police, and though the audience knows the Fireflies are torturous killers, they are framed as the victims in this film. Zombie gets the audience to root for the Fireflies, even after all the horrible torture and murder we saw them commit in the first film.

The film starts with the Firefly family running from the law, as evidence of over seventy-five murders is found on their property. Mother Firefly (Leslie Easterbrook) is arrested and taken to jail. They lose track of Tiny, and Baby and Otis make a run for it. Shortly thereafter, while Otis and Baby are torturing and killing a group of traveling musicians, Captain Spaulding shows up, and we learn that he's Baby's father. Watching the Firefly family on the run is different than watching them in their home. In *House of 1000 Corpses*, they are in their element, their comfort zone. They have all their usual resources and tools, and they have home-field advantage. Out in the world, they are like animals on the run. Scared, prioritizing survival, but backed into a corner, they will fight. Sheriff Wydell (William Forsythe) is taking this case personally, since the Fireflies killed his brother. He wants to hunt them down and make them hurt, not simply arrest them.

It's more action than horror, but *The Devil's Rejects* has plenty of violence and gore. When Baby and Otis are holding the musicians hostage in a motel, Otis shoots one in the head to prove to the other hostages the seriousness of the situation. As the rest are frozen in fear, Otis toys with them, as he did with the tourists in the first film. He forces Gloria (Priscilla Barnes) to strip and perform oral sex on him in front of her husband Roy (Geoffrey Lewis). Otis drags two of the men out to help him find a cache of guns he buried, and when the hostages try to fight back and escape, he kills them, beating Roy to death violently by striking him over and over again in the head. When Sheriff Wydell eventually captures the three remaining Fireflies, he puts them through violent torture, including attaching pictures of their victims to their bodies and leaving them to burn alive. They escape, and Baby running away is an excellent call back to the first film, as someone is now calling her a rabbit and telling her to run, just as Otis did to Mary.

Unlike *House of 1000 Corpses*, *The Devil's Rejects* was created after the Millennial Nasty era was well underway. There is plenty of edgy dialogue that makes it feel of its time, including homophobia, and a very embarrassing conversation about raping a dead chicken (this scene actually felt like it would be more at home in an Eli Roth movie). There is a drawn-out and graphic sex scene, which ends up being a dream, and ultimately doesn't add anything to the movie except a sex scene. *The Devil's Rejects* takes the opportunity to lean into the gritty color palette of the time, whereas that wasn't a trend yet when *House of 1000 Corpses* was made. The holding cell where the cops are keeping Mother Firefly and the scene in which Wydell is torturing the other Fireflies would be right at home in the *Saw* or *Hostel* franchises.

More than a decade later, a third film to finish the trilogy was directed by Rob Zombie and released in 2019, *3 from Hell.* It appears that the Firefly family dies at the end of *The Devil's Rejects,* but the third film reveals how they survived. The third film didn't do as well as the first two because fans felt it was watered down and inauthentic to the Firefly family. Perhaps so many years later, fans' tastes had changed, too.

## *Repo! The Genetic Opera* (2008)

"I will stop at nothing to keep you safe."

If you haven't heard of or haven't thought of *Repo!* In a while, it's probably not your fault. In my opinion, this film doesn't get nearly the attention it deserves. It's a nasty, gruesome body horror that also happens to be a musical. The breathtaking singing makes up for the imperfect CGI. The music is influenced by the popular music of the time, namely nu-metal, but that makes it feel like a perfect Millennial Nasty.

There are two families at the center of this story: the Wallace family and the Largos. Nathan Wallace (Anthony Head) is Shilo's (Alexa PenaVega) father, and he raises her on his own, after her mother died years ago. Nathan told Shilo she has the same disease her mother did, and he keeps her inside and on a strict regimen of mystery medicine. The Largos are the wealthiest and most powerful family in this film's not-too-distant futuristic hellscape. They run a company called GeneCo, which finances surgeries, designed to keep people in medical debt. Unbeknownst to Shilo, her father works for the Largos as the Repo Man, ripping out organs when people fall behind on their payments.

Like any good (soap) opera, the families are more complicated than they seem, and secret relationships are revealed throughout the film. Rotti Largo (Paul Sorvino), the patriarch, is trying to decide which of his children should inherit GeneCo:

Luigi (Bill Moseley), who has a bad temper combined with a strong sexual appetite; Parvi (Kevin 'ohGr' Ogilvie), who is only interested in himself and constantly replacing and changing his face; or Amber Sweet (Paris Hilton), who wants to be a famous singer, but is addicted to surgery and the subsequent painkiller, and her life is a mess. Rotti, disappointed with all his children, decides he can leave the business to Shilo, and blow up her life in the process by revealing many secrets: Rotti was involved with Shilo's mother before she met Shilo's father; Shilo has a godmother in Blind Mag (Sarah Brightman), the most famous singer and the face of GeneCo; that Shilo's father is the Repo Man; and maybe worst of all, that she's never been sick, that her father has been lying to her. In a case of Munchausen's by proxy, Nathan was drugging Shilo to keep her weak and keeping her home to ostensibly protect her from the world. Talk about fucked up families. There are no role models here. Each family is full of secrets, lies, and disappointment.

But how could a musical soap opera be a Millennial Nasty? *Repo!* proves itself with bleakness and violence. This film capitalizes on the cultural fears of the time that our systems would fail, and we would lose everything. In *Repo!*, the medical systems have failed so spectacularly, it's like America's current opioid crisis on steroids. People are addicted to surgery, and their culture encourages it. In our present society, it's not that different from the way beauty products are sold - hate yourself and buy this product to fix it. GeneCo is set up to take your money or kill you if you can't pay. This plot reflects a fear of capitalism during a bad recession in 2008. In *Repo!*, one family with the most money controls everything, and all others are at their mercy. The poor masses will die. For Americans without much money, that is a relatable fear. And of course, organ repossession is plenty gory and violent. The gritty aesthetic with the bleak view of the future gives us a perfect Millennial Nasty... plus original songs.

## *The Loved Ones* (2009)

> "It's always been you, daddy. Just you
> and me."

*The Loved Ones* (Dir. Sean Byrne) focuses on Australian teenagers Brent (Xavier Samuel), Holly (Victoria Thaine), and Lola Stone (Robin McLeavy). Brent and Holly are a couple, and when Lola asks Brent to the spring school dance, he politely declines. Lola and her father (John Brumpton) kidnap Brent before the dance and bring him to their home for an evening of torture in formal clothes. The complete story takes its time to unfold, so the audience really has to sit with the strange and uncomfortable, becoming more and more horrifying. But it's immediately obvious that Lola and her father have a disturbing relationship, and while the film never shows them engaging in incest, it's heavily implied. Lola's mother, who everyone calls Bright Eyes (Anne Scott-Pendlebury), is a brain-dead torture victim who is propped up at the table in a formal dress. Lola and her father keep similar victims in a crawl space under their house, where they hide their torture victims after drilling holes in their brains and pouring acid into their heads.

Lola carries the film, and the actress's performance is outstanding. The character of Lola is straightforward but complex. She acts highly immature for her age - her bedroom is decorated like that of a young girl, not a teenager. Everything that can be pale pink is pale pink. Her speech and mannerisms seem like she is playing the part of a little girl. She has several dolls posed in tableaus of different sexual positions, and the contrast between a young child's toy and adult sex acts is unsettling. The way her father leers at her - especially while he watches her try on her pink dress for the dance - implies maybe she stopped mentally developing at the age her dad started abusing her. The movie leaves it unclear. It's easy to think Lola would be lonely and bullied - her name is an anagram of "lost alone" - but we don't see that in the film. The only time we see her interacting outside her home, she is asking Brent to the dance. He is kind when he says no and explains that he already has a date. Whoever Lola is, however she acts, it seems driven by her home life rather than her peers.

She pits her father against her mother in bids for his attention, which is unnecessary, because her mother can't speak or move on her own. But Lola can't stand her father looking at another woman, and she acts like a spoiled child. It's the inverse of what she does with the boys she brings home to torture, which she had done many times before kidnapping Brent. She taunts her father by interacting with the boys, flirting with them and sitting on their laps in between tortures, and makes her father earn her attention. She tells her father she can't find a boyfriend because "he's her prince." Even if they weren't torturing and murdering, they would be a horrific family. After Brent escapes his ties and stabs her father to death, Lola smothers her mother. Lola has no use for Bright Eyes now that she doesn't need to use her to get her father's attention.

The Stone family raises many comparisons to the family in *The Texas Chain Saw Massacre* (1974). They torture together, as a family, around a dinner table with their victim tied to a chair. The Stone family eating dinner is disgusting enough, without the addition of torture and violence. They are eating chicken on the bone, sucking the grease off their fingers, and Lola shoves it into her mother's face. They are also drinking milk, and Lola chugs a full glass, leaving milk around the edges of her lips, to bully Brent into urinating into her glass. After she threatens to nail his penis to the chair - or rather, that her father will - she goes to put her mouth on his penis, with milk still on her face, though he just finished urinating. To round it out, Lola screams in his face, ordering Brent to cry, while she hammers into his feet. All those disgusting elements stacking up on top of a torture scene bring to mind the dinner table scene in *The Texas*

*Chain Saw Massacre* (1974). It's a wonderful homage to a classic Video Nasty.

The title *The Loved Ones* carries abundant meaning, because this film is all about family. Apart from the Stone family, we meet two other families in pain. The film opens with Brent driving a car, and getting into an accident that kills his father. He and his mother (Victoria Eagger) are understandably grieving. Brent wears a razor blade on a chain like a necklace and cuts himself with it when he is in emotional pain. His mother is trying to keep an eye on him, but accidentally pushing him away by being overprotective. They don't communicate well, and it's heartbreaking to see. Similarly, the Valentine family is hurting. The Valentines have two teenage kids: Timmy (Stephen Walden), who went missing, and Mia (Jessica McNamee), who is grieving the loss of her brother, and coping with sex, drugs, and alcohol. Unbeknownst to the Valentines, Timmy is missing because Lola captured him. Timmy's and Mia's father is a police officer, feeling like he failed his family and community by not finding his son. There is no trace of him. When Brent is reported missing, he makes it his personal responsibility to find him. There is a scene with Mia crying in bed, and she says to her father, "Why didn't you find him?" The families and their pain represented in this film are diverse and realistic, giving a rawness to this nasty film.

*The Loved Ones* came out near the end of the decade, as the trends were about to shift into trauma-focused horror, and it feels like a perfect bridge between the two eras. But it's exactly in line with Millennial Nasties. It's violent in creative ways, which was getting harder to do with each passing year offering more violent films. The story keeps the audience guessing, since the viewer has Brent's point of view as he figures out what's happening to him. The mix of sex and violence is the right amount of disturbing. *The Loved Ones* goes to lengths other Millennial Nasties didn't, and we have Australia to thank for that.

## RED CORN SYRUP IS THICKER THAN WATER

Horror audiences love to see a fucked-up family. We wanted May to take her mother's terrible lessons and "make" a friend. We wanted the Fireflies to survive and escape the police. We hoped Shilo and her dad would reconcile. We were captivated by Lola Stone.

In more recent years, horror film families can still be fucked up, but the approach is more nuanced and often sadder. There has been a focus on aging, mental illness, and psychological and generational trauma in movies such as *The Babadook* (Dir. Jennifer Kent 2014), *The Invitation* (Dir. Karyn Kusama, 2015), *The Witch* (Dir. Robert Eggers, 2015), *Get Out* (Dir. Jordan Peele, 2017), and *Hereditary* (Dir. Ari Aster, 2018). And the year 2019 proved that audiences are not looking for families like the Fireflies anymore, at least not for now.

A fucked-up family might be better than no family at all. Otherwise, you might end up as a...

# SINGLE TRAPPED FEMALE

Cᴀᴘᴛɪᴠɪᴛʏ **(2007)** ᴀɴᴅ **P2 (2007)**

Two films of the time, less popular than some of their peers, take different approaches to similar stories. Trapping and victimizing women has been a hallmark of the horror story for centuries, and the Millennial Nasty era was no different. Both films in this chapter tell a classic story of women trapped by men, ultimately for sex and mind games, and tortured in isolation. Similar to the *Punish the Bitches* chapter later in this book, the women in *Single Trapped Female* films are punished for their perceived sins, which sometimes include simply existing. Unlike slashers, these stories are each focused on one woman, and all the torture is directed at her. Both the protagonists in these films fight like hell to make it out and survive, but at what cost?

## *Captivity* **(2007)**

> "I've been stalked, I know creeps, it comes
> with the job."

*Captivity* (Dir. Roland Joffé) isn't as popular as some of the other films covered in this book, but it deserves its place on the Millennial Nasty list. It's an original story with plenty of gore. Jennifer (Elisha Cuthbert) is a beautiful but cold model - guarded, but not shrinking. She says what she thinks, whether others like it or not. She's famous enough to have her ads on city buses and she's always giving interviews. But it's lonely at the top. Her only friend is her little dog, Suzy. One night, alone at a bar waiting for a friend, she's drugged and kidnapped. She wakes up in a basement cell, unaware of how she got there. She reacts with anger, not fear, shouting and demanding to be released. She's subjected to a series of horrible tortures, but shortly, she learns that there is another cell next to hers, housing a man. A hunky, sweet man, at that. Gary (Daniel Gillies) is his name, and they try to escape together a few times. But there is a reveal, later in the film, that Gary is kidnapping women with his brother Ben (Pruitt Taylor Vince). They regularly kidnap, torture, rape, and then murder women, and make tapes and scrapbooks to keep the memories forever. Eventually Jennifer escapes, and in the alternate ending on the unrated DVD, she becomes a vigilante, killing men who hurt women.

Based on the plot alone, there doesn't need to be much defending of this as a Millennial Nasty. It's often classified as torture porn. But there is something so nasty in the treatment of Jennifer. All the brothers' sick energy pointed at one person at a time, and Jennifer is tortured both psychologically and physi-cally. Jennifer is captured when she's drinking alone at a bar. Her drink is drugged before it's even served to her, but it's a nod to the way women can be blamed for not watching their drinks and for going out alone. A magazine calls her "the girl with no heart," because if she's an intense, career-focused woman, she must not be capable of love. As the story progresses and she falls for Gary, or the fake version of himself he is presenting, it's as if she has opened her heart to love. She is ultimately punished for her vulnerability, as she falls victim to Gary's and Ben's mind games.

She is forced to watch tapes of interviews she gave, and in one, mentions enjoying attention from older men since she was a teenager. There is a dirty secret in our culture, and probably lots of cultures around the world, that near-childlike youth is attractive in women and girls. It's desirable for men to pursue and date women younger than themselves, and this can become predatory quickly. Teenage girls, who are not yet adults, are encouraged to cover up, and they are blamed for the way men look at them. Cultural implications teach girls to appreciate and crave attention from older men, rather than to be cautious of it. This can lead to young women and girls being preyed upon by men, and not knowing how to respond or who they should tell. If Jennifer has been harassed from such a young age, it's not surprising she would be protective of herself as an adult.

The backstory of Gary and Ben includes sexual abuse at the hands of their mother. They rewatch a tape of their mother apologizing to Gary, after sexually abusing him, while Ben watches from the doorframe. On the tape, Gary stabs his mother to death, takes a Polaroid picture, and smiles. As an adult, he watches this tape while holding his mother's nightgown. The boys' dynamic continues into their adult actions, and Gary is the one who interacts with the women they kidnap and tricks them into sex, while Ben watches and arranges the scrapbooks. When Jennifer realizes the extent of their childhood abuse, she pleads for her life to Gary by saying, "I am not your mother." It's similar to Beth's pleas in *Hostel 2* (2007) when she tells Stuart, "I am not your wife." Both movies involve men wanting to kill women who remind them of something they don't want to think about. What the boys went through as children is horrible, and the viewer can feel sympathy for them, but they are choosing their actions as adults. The film is not using the abuse as an excuse for their actions, but rather using it as a plot point to make its twist more complex.

ARIEL POWERS-SCHAUB

The nastiness of this film is both onscreen and implied. The level of gore matched the torture porn standard of the time. Jennifer is forced to watch a video of another woman's face melted off with acid, and the camera holds the shot as her skin melts off her skull. There is a scene in which she must choose between killing herself or killing her dog. She is forced to shoot her dog with a shotgun, splattering guts all over the clear cage that was holding Suzy. In one of the nastiest torture scenes, she is force-fed a smoothie made of body parts. After all the gore is blended together, it's bright red, and poured down her throat in a funnel. She's gagging and vomiting it back up into the funnel, but has to drink it all. Ben then takes some gore from the side of her mouth and puts it on himself like lipstick. Jennifer is also tortured in less bloody ways. They trap her in a glass box, and it seems like she's about to drown in sand until she escapes. Once, when she wakes up after being drugged, her face is bandaged. As she removes the bandages, shaking in fear, she finds a fake wound on her face, and she's not been physically harmed. They are using makeup, a tool she uses every day in her success, against her as special effects. When you consider the full scope of what Gary and Ben are doing to women - kidnapping, tricking, and raping women - it's awful enough without the psychological torture. It's a complicated, convoluted mind game.

The filmmaking is also evident of the Millennial Nasty era and particularly looks like it was influenced by the *Saw* films. The stony cell where Jennifer is trapped could be one of Jigsaw's chambers. Similarly, there are a variety of devices designed only for torture, and I wouldn't be surprised if Ben and Gary had interned under John Kramer in some shared universe. There is green and yellow lighting during the nastiest, goriest parts of the film. Before the killer is revealed, his features are hidden, as were Jigsaw's, and there is a huge plot twist that changes everything, just like in *Saw*. In another parallel to *Hostel 2*, Jennifer escapes after shooting Gary in the crotch (and then

68

shooting him a few more times for good measure). An aspect of *Captivity* that's uniquely its own comes from the scrapbooks.

There are several shots in the film in which Ben is cutting words out of magazines to add to his torture memory books, the way a different movie villain might cut words and letters to make a ransom note. Instead, however, these words are placed into a torture scrapbook. The welcoming look of the scrapbooking scenes contrasted with the grimy, dark basement, gives this film an intentionally uncomfortable imbalance.

Somewhat underseen, Captivity is a nasty film appreciated by gorehounds who eat up everything from this era.

### *P2* (2007)

> "Those guys always do whatever they
> want."

*P2* (Dir. Franck Khalfoun) is another story of a career-focused woman getting preyed upon by a man, though the story unfolds differently than in *Captivity*. Angela (Rachel Nichols) is a successful business professional, with a sensible button-down shirt and her hair in a tight bun. She's working late on Christmas Eve, and she's trying to get out the door in time to see her family. Her parents, sister, niece, and nephew are waiting for her to show up with the Santa suit and armfuls of presents. She heads down to the nearly empty parking garage, and her car won't start. Thomas (Wes Bentley), the eager and helpful, but almost too helpful, security guard pops up, and tries to jump her car. When that doesn't work, she calls a cab, but she's locked inside the building and the cab leaves before she can find anyone to unlock the door for her. As she's trying to decide what to do next, Thomas knocks her out with chloroform and carries her away to his office. When she wakes, she's in a formal white dress, with her hair down and a fresh face of makeup, chained to a chair. Thomas suggests they have dinner and tries to make normal conversation with the woman he has trapped. The rest of the film follows Angela and Thomas in a game of cat-and-mouse, as Angela tries desperately to escape, any way she can, and Thomas reveals how unhinged he is.

*Captivity* was a movie focused on punishing women for being beautiful, being assertive, and taking care of themselves - and, of course, for drinking alone at a bar. *P2* is about punishing a woman who is too focused on her career to have a partner or children, or even see her existing family. We never hear what Angela thinks of her own life, we just hear through Thomas's perspective that she can't possibly be happy in her circumstances. Angela might be happy with her life. One of the ways she tries to appeal to Thomas to let her go is by lying to say that she has a boyfriend. This is a common tactic women use to deflect unwanted attention from men. That often works because if a man won't respect a woman, maybe he will respect a man, and back off from another man's "property". Angela is not so lucky here, and Thomas doesn't believe her.

*P2* offers an exploration of victim-blaming. Angela is so focused on work that she walks to the parking garage by herself after dark, something a woman would almost certainly be victim-blamed for. Even though she follows common safety measures, such as carrying a cell phone, taking the elevator down with the building guard and calling a cab because she knows that will be safer than dealing with her car in an empty garage - she is still victimized. Women shouldn't have to take every possible safety measure, but if they don't, people will often imply their victimization is somehow a woman's own fault. Angela could not have accounted for the parking structure security staff to be stalking her and planning this for months. But someone looking at her situation after the fact might wonder why she accepted help from Thomas at all. Even when women are vigilant to the dangers of the world, sometimes all they can do is never enough.

Angela remains exceptionally tough throughout the film and

tries everything she can to escape. When pleading and lying don't work, she stabs Thomas with a fork, runs to one of the gates, and yells for help. She eventually eludes him and recovers her cell phone and loses a fingernail trying to call emergency services while leaning as far as she can outside, trying to get cell phone service. She remains handcuffed for most of the time. She is running from Thomas (real handcuffs on the actress, by the way), hiding, and defending herself with anything she can find. This is skilled storytelling, but it's also an example of cultural expectation. Women, when trapped or cornered by men, are supposed to fight for their survival. Even though it would be understandable to totally freeze, and just wait for someone to come look for you, the victim blaming is worse if you don't fight at every possible moment.

There is a second man in the film who has harassed Angela, although her interactions with him and Thomas are profoundly different. Her coworker Jim (Simon Reynolds), who appears older than her, visits her office near the beginning of the film to offer what seems like a sincere, if poorly delivered, apology. He says he had too many drinks at the Christmas party and things got out of hand. Angela handles it purposefully - she's cold but professional. She accepts his apology without soothing his feelings, and she doesn't brush off the seriousness of it. For an incident that never should have happened, it seems like Jim and Angela are both determined to move forward from it. Thomas has a recording of the assault taking place in the elevator, and he shows it to Angela before giving her his "Christmas present," Jim tied to a chair in the lower level of the garage. Thomas insists that he needs to protect Angela, and despite her pleas, violently kills Jim because he treated Angela like a "slut." Thomas is clearly thinking about his own feelings, not Angela's. If he really was trying to help Angela, he would have respected her pleas not to kill Jim.

There is enough onscreen, visible nastiness to put this film in the Millennial Nasty category, though *P2* is not usually classified as torture porn. When Jim is killed, crushed against a wall with a car, his guts flop out of him, and his skull explodes. When Angela eventually has to kill Thomas's guard dog, Rocky, she is brutal with a tire iron and ends up covered in blood. Angela discovers that Thomas videotaped her when she was passed out and is saying disturbing things to her while dressing her and fondling her without her consent. Understandably, that causes Angela to scream and smash the TV instead of watching the rest of the video.

Much of the torture in this film is psychological. It shows the insidious ways men can convince themselves they are "nice guys, just trying to help" and end up treating women horribly. Thomas's words and actions are realistic. As soon as Angela asks for help, he's putting her down and gaslighting her. He convinces her not to call for a cab at first, and when jumping her car doesn't work, he "jokingly" invites her to stay for dinner. When she shows frustration at the clearly frustrating situation, he tells her, "You should be grateful, it's the holidays." As if she's never allowed to show any sign of unhappiness around him. He takes her frustration personally and says, over and over again, "I was just trying to help." All his lines have enough plausible deniability, they could be said by someone with Angela's best interests in mind. This is a ploy that traps women. If women go along with this "niceness" and end up in a bad situation, they are blamed for not noticing the creepiness and removing themselves from the situation. If they trust their instincts and try to protect themselves, they are told they are overreacting. Thomas creates a classic, impossible situation for Angela, and then chains her to a table when she resists more than he thought she would.

Because *P2* is not exactly torture porn, it doesn't have all the filmmaking hallmarks that many other Millennial Nasties do. While it's gritty and gruesome at times, it uses more blue lighting than green or yellow, and it feels more like a slasher in the scenes in which Thomas is stalking Angela in the garage.

Her white dress is even similar to the white tank tops Final Girls were wearing at the time. There are occasional shots through security cameras, which lend a creepy, voyeuristic feeling of being watched. The excellent performances of the two main actors add to the tension. Nichols does an excellent job of portraying how Angela must be feeling - it's stressful watching her walk around with armfuls of gifts while she's looking for help to jump her car then call a cab, and for most of the film, she's in an impractical dress and barefoot, running around a concrete structure in the winter. The entire film, the viewer, can feel Angela's burden. Bentley also delivers a chilling, horrifying performance as Thomas, the guy you might know who turns out to be a predator.

Despite its straightforward premise, it's actually a niche combination of factors - it's not quite a slasher, not quite torture porn, and much of American horror at the time could be classified as one or the other. It has similarities to a home invasion but lacks the fear of your domestic safety being invaded. Thankfully, with the advent of streaming and social media, this Millennial Nasty is earning the following it deserves from the fans who it was made for.

The ending is the perfect combo of nastiness and catharsis to wrap up the story. After what feels like an endless chase, culminating with Angela and Thomas, both in cars driving at each other in a game of chicken, she stabs him in the eye and chokes him. She unlocks her handcuffs and cuffs him to a car, taking his keys to escape. He's yelling after her, "Why can't we be friends? Why can't we spend Christmas together? Do you hear me, you stupid fucking cunt?" She slowly turns, sets fire to the gasoline leaking from the car wreck, and sets Thomas ablaze as he screams in pain. She's walking out of the parking garage, under the automatic sprinklers, washing away blood and her sins, so she can emerge into the early morning pure again in her now-dirty white dress. She's limping down the road, as snow falls, when fire trucks pull up and stop for her. She made it out alive.

## DON'T BLAME THE VICTIM.

*Captivity* and *P2* are the prefect pair of Millennial Nasties. Two women, married to their work, who each have to kill a dog for survival. The men in the movies have similar goals, but they justify themselves and go about their plans differently. In both films, the women are supposed to just give in, and give up hope at the optimal time for their captors. We can never know if Jennifer and Angela were blamed for their own victimization after the fact, and all we know about Jennifer is that she becomes a vigilante killer. Even if women fight for their freedom, what happens to them once they are free? That question was not explored much in this nasty era. At least they both survived.

# PART TWO

ORIGINAL SLASHERS

# LIFE AFTER SCREAM

## SLASHERS GET NASTY

In 1996, Wes Craven's *Scream* breathed new life into horror, and especially into slashers. Updating the familiar slasher tropes established through the 1980s with modern understanding and acknowledging the "rules to survive a slasher film" explained by Dr. Carol Clover gave filmmakers fresh ideas to play with. This led to a late '90s slasher boom, and the rest of the slashers looked and felt a lot like *Scream*. They were slick, stylish, witty, and had sexy actors we knew from TV shows. Trends take time to change, and that means the slasher trends carried into the 2000s. But filmmakers had to attract audiences who were becoming hungrier for gritty, nasty violence, which couldn't be more different from *Scream*.

Scream was influenced by '70s and '80s slashers, and film-makers in the 2000s were often influenced by '70s and 80s Giallo and exploitation films. Millennial Nasty filmmakers were, of course, aware of *Scream*, but likely their filmmaking aspirations came long before *Scream* did. Millennial Nasty slashers are unlike any from another era. In the 2000s, we were treated to original slashers that did familiar things - killers in the woods, cannibals, road trips, groups of young friends - but filtered through brutal violence and nastiness. The kills of this decade were no longer "masked man slashes you and you fall down" like the slashers of the '70s and '80s. Now teenagers and young adults were being crushed, burned, dismembered, and eaten. The slashers analyzed in this section all spawned franchises that allowed the movies to go bigger and nastier each time. Come on, let's chop it up.

# STAY ON THE PATH

WRONG TURN (2003), WRONG TURN 2 (2007), HATCHET
(2006) AND HATCHET 2 (2010)

Getting lost in rural areas and young people going where they
aren't supposed to have always been classic setups for slasher
films. Every summer camp movie set in the woods, every time
teens sneak off to investigate a haunted or abandoned building
to drink and have sex, we can be sure a large, looming figure
will emerge from the dark to kill them brutally. The *Hatchet* and
*Wrong Turn* films are no exception to the slasher formula, but
they have the Millennial Nasty flavor. They both take place in
unique locations and include beautiful nature shots juxtaposed
with the grisly killings. And while they follow slasher rules,
they also break a lot of those rules. The post-*Scream* (1996)
copycat slashers were waning, but nastier slashers were
sneaking in to take their place.

## *Wrong Turn* (2003)

> "West Virginia, trespassing, not a great
> combination."

*Wrong Turn,* directed by Rob Schmidt, is a slasher that came out early in the Millennial Nasty decade, in 2003. *Wrong Turn* follows a group of young friends, ages unclear, who are camping in the woods in West Virginia. Similar to the setups in *Hostel* (2005) and *Hatchet* (2006), they are going on a camping trip because the Final Girl Jessie (Eliza Dushku) was dumped by her boyfriend. Her friends aren't that excited about being in the woods, but Jessie loves the outdoors, and her friends are trying to lift her spirits. They get into a car accident with Chris (Desmond Harrington), who was on the back roads to avoid highway traffic and try to make it to a job interview on time. Without a vehicle or a cell phone signal, four of them hike to try to find a phone or anyone to help, and that's when they stumble upon a family of cannibals.

The film uses a classic slasher template for its characters and setup. There is an opening kill of characters we don't spend much time with, and Jessie is clearly telegraphed as our Final Girl from the beginning, in her white tank top. She is recently single, she is loyal to her friends, she is practical and thoughtful of others, and she is smart and capable. There is a "party couple," Evan (Kevin Zegers) and Francine (Lindy Booth), who are rude to everyone and stay behind to have sex and smoke pot while the others go look for help. They are, predictably, the next to be killed. There is a sweet couple, Carly (Emmanuelle Chriqui) and Scott (Jeremy Sisto), who just got engaged, and while somewhat annoying in their public displays of affection, we hope they survive (but we know they will die). The only survivors are Jessie, the final girl, and Chris, the mature, level-headed outsider who comes to her rescue. This movie even has the holy grail of slasher icons - a gas station harbinger, who tries to warn Chris not to take the back roads. There is a nod to the meta-horror *Scream* brought to slashers by having the characters be genre savvy. When the group finds the cannibals' house in the woods, Scott references *Deliverance* (1972). They decide after shockingly little debate to walk right in and look for a phone, even though no one is answering the door. Often in slashers, especially those referencing *The Texas Chain Saw Massacre* (1974), young people move through the world like they own the place.

What makes this film a sign of things to come throughout the decade is how brutal and violent it is. The cannibals' house is covered in filth, and the lighting in the interior scenes makes it appear even grimier than it is. When the friends first enter the house, they spend a few minutes looking around. There are dishes, remnants of old food, and scraps of dead things everywhere. A stock pot is boiling on the stove, bubbling something mysterious, dark and chunky. The toilet is as disgusting as you would expect, and there are jars of body parts around the house and in the fridge, including a jar of jawbones. The final straw for the friends is finding a human body in the bathtub, but of course, that's the moment the cannibals come home, and the friends have to hide. The house is by far the nastiest part of the film - very different from the clean homes and good schools of the '90s slashers. The kills are nasty for a slasher - that is to say, compared to some other films discussed in this book, these kills are nothing special. But compared to the history of slashers, in which teenagers were often stabbed, sometimes off screen, *Wrong Turn* offers more gore. For example, Francine is garroted by barbed wire and Carly's head is chopped in half.

And, of course, the family of cannibals. As *Wrong Turn* became a franchise, the lore around the cannibals and where they came from expanded. But the first movie doesn't explain much, and in it the cannibals don't speak, so both the characters and the audience are left with no understanding. The cannibals communicate by making clicking sounds and cackling, and they move through the woods quickly and stealthily. They are three men, all dressed in dirty clothes and missing fingers, teeth, and hair. The cannibals do not care how they are perceived by other people, possibly because they see others as food, and we don't normally care what our food thinks of us. There is no attempt to hide their crimes. They are not shy about the graveyard of tourists' cars they have on their property, or the personal items collected from their victims. Because we cannot understand the cannibal family's motives or communication, they are "othered" by default. *Wrong Turn* is a franchise about fear of The Other; fear of what we don't understand. That has always been a topic ripe for exploration through the horror genre, and especially in the early 2000s when America was so distrustful of anyone we considered The Other.

### *Wrong Turn 2: Dead End* (2007)

> "You don't wanna be out in them woods at
> night."

*Wrong Turn 2: Dead End*, directed by Joe Lynch, joyfully leaned into the horror trends of the time, and while it is another cannibal slasher, this movie is even nastier than its predecessor. It takes place near the location of the first movie but doesn't have a direct connection other than the cannibal family. From the opening kill, the film feels more irreverent and fun. Kim (Kimberly Caldwell) is driving an expensive-looking car in the middle of nowhere, yelling at her agent on a Bluetooth headset, when she hits one of the cannibals and gets out of the car to check on him. She is chopped in half through the crotch, intestines spilling into the street, and dragged away in two pieces by the cannibal family. Immediately we know the gore has increased from the original, as has the self-awareness and silliness.

The rest of the film follows a group of wannabe celebrities prepping for an outdoor survival reality TV show, including all the personalities you would see on such a show. We were enamored with reality TV during this time period, and audiences treated it as escapist fun, so it makes for a perfect backdrop for a Millennial Nasty. Mara (Aleksa Palladino) is a producer, and her boyfriend Michael (Matthew Currie Holmes), recently going by "M," is the director. He's an egotistic jerk, and she is shy and under-confident. Elena (Yan-Kay Crystal Lowe) brings the sex appeal, while Jonesy (Steve Braun) seems like the jokester who takes things too far and harasses all the women. Jake (Texas Battle) was a rising star in football, until he injured his shoulder, and he's seeking a new path. Nina (Erica Leerhsen) is an assertive, outspoken vegan, who seems to seek out confrontation for fun. The host Dale (Henry Rollins) is an ex-Marine who pretends to have a hardened heart but is actually kind and empathetic. Amber (Daniella Alonso) quickly becomes his favorite, as she's also an ex-Marine, and was disowned by her parents for being queer.

The premise of the show is that it's post-apocalypse, "the government is no longer in control," literally the end of the world, and do you have what it takes to survive? The name is Ultimate Survivalist, or U.S. for short. It's a clear allegory for the fear America was still feeling after 9/11, but how we also compartmentalized, and leaned into reality TV to escape actual reality. The structure of a reality show gives the film a clever way to get around cell phones - they are taken away from the contestants at the beginning of the show, so there is no question as to why they can't call the police when the cannibals show up. The setup also allows for some creative filmmaking, including POV shots from head cams on the contestants, and scenes shot "for TV" with multiple cameras and overly dramatic zooms and music cues.

This film has more of everything than the first film - more sex, more gore, and more backstory of the cannibals and how far their influence reaches. One character sitting alone in a cabin, who happens to be the gas station harbinger from the first film, explains that jobs were lost in the area when the mill was shut down, leaving the locals in poverty, and their desperation lead them to cannibalism. Around the same time, there was a toxic spill in the river, leading to birth defects. There are female cannibals included this time, one of whom gives birth on a table in an awfully graphic scene. In fact, the cannibal family is overtly sexual in *Wrong Turn 2*, one of them masturbating watching Elena tan on the beach, and who is then joined by his sister for sex after killing and scalping Elena. There is much more torture inflicted by cannibals in this one, as they play with their food, and they even speak a few words in this film, in addition to the secret language of clicks we heard in the first film.

In its ninety-seven-minute run time, with a cast of killable characters, there is a surprising amount of character development for a slasher. While there are still slasher movie tropes - sex equals death, for example - there are added twists. The quiet, good-girl producer, Mara, whose director boyfriend is cheating on her, is expected to be the Final Girl. She keeps insisting she will be terrible at the show's game and won't "survive," meaning she would be eliminated based on the show's rules. After Mara and Nina narrowly escape the cannibals' home (through their toilet-closet floor, disgustingly), Mara gets an ax to the head. When she dies, we are left with Nina, the antisocial one. It's unusual to save a character who is less likable, especially a female character. Like the first film, this film has two survivors, and the only other survivor is Jake, shirking another slasher trope of killing a Black character first (or at all). There is also a twist with the harbinger character - he ends up being one of the elder cannibals and tries to kill Dale.

The gender and racial politics in this film are not at all perfect, but they were relatively progressive for the time. Jonesy starts out disgusting, sexually harassing everyone, especially Amber. Amber explains that she's a lesbian, and Jonesy doesn't immediately start treating her with respect, but at least he stops harassing her. After she saves his life, he apologizes, and says he's "never going to diss her or any woman ever again." Sadly, he dies shortly after. Amber refuses to leave him behind as he gets stuck in a trap, owing to her background as a Marine, and their death is surprisingly moving. They comfort one another as they swing from a tree, and the cannibal father and son use them as target practice. Jake, the football player who blew out his rotator cuff, has to further injure his shoulder to save Nina, putting his football career even farther out of reach. He seems selfish at the start of the film, and he sacrifices something important to save another person who was rude to him. Nina also makes some tough choices. She covers scars on her wrists from when she tried to kill herself after her fiancé cheated on her. But she has to injure herself again to survive, twisting her arms free from barbed wire restraints, and creating new scars. She is a staunch vegan, but she has to bite a cannibal's neck to survive. Though Nina's boundaries are important to her, she chooses when to bend the rules for survival. *Wrong Turn 2* represents so much of pop culture in America at the time. Soldiers were heroes, and could do no wrong, and both Amber and Dale live up to that expectation. Dale frees Jake and Nina from their ties and takes several arrows to the chest so they can escape.

It went straight to video and made good money, as this was a time when DVDs and special features were extremely popular, before streaming was a household convenience. Skipping a theatrical release also meant they didn't have to fight for a specific rating. This film feels more like torture porn than the first one, and it's in the thick of the Millennial Nasty decade. Influenced by slashers that came before, but doing its own nasty thing, *Wrong Turn 2* is a perfect time capsule. The series went on to have several more sequels, including one more in this decade, *Wrong Turn 3: Left for Dead* (Dir. Declan O'Brien, 2009). Future *Wrong Turn* movies get sillier and more fun, and there was a reboot of the first film in 2021, since rebooting horror franchises popular in the 2020s. The first two films in the *Wrong Turn* series remain excellent examples of Millennial Nasties.

### *Hatchet* (2006)

> "Ya'll don't even know where you are."

The *Hatchet* films take place in the swamps of New Orleans, Louisiana, in a swampy area simply called "the bayou." Specifically, it takes place in Honey Island Swamp. The bayou is creepy on its own, and it made for a unique slasher setting. Adam Green wrote and directed the first, second and fourth films in the franchise, and he wrote the third film, but it was directed by BJ McDonnell. McDonnell had been a camera operator on the first two films, as well as several other Millennial Nasties mentioned in this book. In other words, the *Hatchet* franchise had creative consistency throughout its run, and Green's vision was brought to life on screen through the hard work he and others put into the films.

*Hatchet* tells the audience exactly what kind of movie it will be right away. After the first kill, which is a brutal slaughter of a father and son hunting alligators at night, there is a Marilyn Manson song playing over a debaucherous montage of Bourbon Street in New Orleans during Mardi Gras. There are more breasts than I could bother to count, just in the first few minutes of the movie. The party scene feels overwhelming and a bit disgusting, with drinking and puking and making out all blurred together. We're swiftly introduced to a group of young male friends, who took a trip to help Ben (Joel David Moore) move past a recent breakup. It's reminiscent of the setup for *Hostel* (2005), down to the details of Ben's friends trying to badger him into drinking and sex that he's not interested in. Instead, Ben and a reluctant Marcus (Deon Richmond) go off on their own to take a guided ghost tour of a swamp at night. They meet several other tourists, and a local, Marybeth (Amara

Zaragoza, credited as Tamara Feldman), who is looking for her missing father and brother (the hunters from the opening of the film). The group of tourists learn the local legend of Victor Crowley (Kane Hodder), who was born with birth defects and facial disfigurements, and after being accidentally killed by his own father, haunts the woods and kills anyone who dares to trespass.

It was thrilling to see a completely original and unique slasher franchise that was willing to break the rules. Though the franchise becomes Marybeth's story, the first *Hatchet* film is through Ben's perspective, rather than a Final Girl's. Viewers familiar with horror tropes might assume that Marcus, who is Black, would be the first of the main cast to die, as horror's tendency to kill Black characters first is well-documented. And Marcus does die, but he makes it almost the entire film. Instead, a sweet old white couple are the first to die from the cast of main characters. They are in love; they are interested in meeting others and are excited to be on vacation. And they are taken apart, very literally, by Victor Crowley.

It's clear that Adam Green is a horror fan, and he incorporates several horror icons throughout the franchise. In *Hatchet*, Robert Englund plays one of the victims in the opening kill, and Englund is best known to horror fans as Freddy Krueger in the *Nightmare on Elm Street* franchise. Tony Todd plays an important local tour guide named Reverend Zombie, and he's well-known for his role in *Candyman* (Dir. Bernard Rose, 1992) as the titular character. And last but not least, Kane Hodder plays two roles in *Hatchet*, acting as both Victor Crowley, and also Victor's father. Though Hodder is no stranger to being in front of the camera, he's usually performing stunts, often in a fire suit. Horror fans fell in love with him when he took over as Jason Voorhees, starting with the seventh *Friday the 13th* film. *Hatchet* includes a kill wherein a body is smashed into a tree, in a nod to the sleeping bag kill in *Friday the 13th Part VII: The New Blood* (Dir. John Carl Buechler, 1988), while Hodder was behind the

Jason mask. Lovingly made, *Hatchet* is a horror film for horror fans. The best thing about the film, and all the *Hatchet* films, are the buckets of blood and gore we are served, and the stunts with Kane Hodder involved. Kills include scenes of tearing off arms, ripping a jaw open, and a head twisting and blood spurting, among other gory deaths. All the kills in *Hatchet* are extended, nasty gore, a love letter to practical effects. Some of the nastiest slasher kills ever are in this film. Additionally, there is an excellent piano and synth theme, which makes it feel modern with a nod to '80s slashers. The end is an abrupt jump scare in the style of *Friday the 13th* (Dir. Sean S. Cunningham, 1980).

What makes *Hatchet* such an obvious Millennial Nasty, other than the violence, is how the characters reflect the time period. The actors' performances are strong, and the direction is good, but the characters are deplorable in a way that's supposed to be funny. It's not that the writing is bad - it's well-written dialogue for awful people! Casual misogyny and bigotry are sprinkled heavily throughout. There is homophobic language in the first five minutes of the movie, as a father shames his son about needing to urinate and not being a good enough hunter. There are misogynistic conversations all through the film, making women sound like objects. The jokes have aged quickly, but they were perfectly in place in this era.

The characters in *Hatchet* fit well into the slasher subgenre. There is a Final Girl, a few characters who make questionable choices that are punished with death, and a humanoid monster in the woods. Victor Crowley is meant to be a sympathetic monster, a common theme in horror since at least the days of *Frankenstein* (Shelley, 1818). Victor was kept away from the world for his physical differences, which ultimately led to his death. It brings to mind the *Friday the 13th* franchise, and the way many fans feel sympathy toward Jason because he was bullied and neglected by camp counselors. Whether or not we should feel sympathy for a violent killer is a topic for another day, but *Hatchet* leans heavily on the audience to ask themselves the question. The young white guy, Ben, is portrayed as the most reasonable person on the tour, if not the most capable. Meanwhile, another charter named Shawn played by Parry Shen gets a much less flattering portrayal. The character is constantly shifting accents, and changing stories about where he's from, to add comedy to the film. It's well done by Shen, but it plays into a horror trope of not being able to trust those who appear different from you.

Marybeth is a straightforward Final Girl. She is somber, reticent, and close with her family. She protects others and is not interested in Ben's advances. The other women in the film are not portrayed so positively. Misty (Mercedes McNab) and Jenna (Joleigh Fiore, credited as Joleigh Fioreavanti) are young women who are hoping to be discovered and kick off acting careers. They are being tricked by a man claiming to be a producer who can get them on a series called Bayou Beavers, a clear reference to *Girls Gone Wild* wherein young women are encouraged to take their clothes off in public for random guys with cameras. Before Misty and Jenna discover they are being tricked, they are almost constantly taking their shirts off. Their characters serve two purposes: Not only are they an excuse to get female nudity into the film, they are examples of "dumb catty mean girls" and we are supposed to cheer for their deaths after laughing at them. They are quite mean to each other, and Misty is portrayed to be especially stupid, with Jenna picking on her and rolling her eyes. They are not pleasant characters to spend time with, but they make sense in this film, at the time it was made. Most of the characters die before they can make it to the sequel, and the abrupt end of *Hatchet* makes it looks like everyone might be dead at the hands of Victor Crowley.

### *Hatchet II* (2010)

"Every now and then, some stupid son of a

bitch thinks he knows better."

*Hatchet II*, again written and directed by Adam Green, was released at the end of the decade. While it was influenced by its time, it also stayed true to its roots as a fresh and original slasher. Like a good sequel, it builds on and expands the lore of the first film, but the nastiness and gore stay about the same. In this film, we learn that Victor Crowley was born when his father had an affair with his mother's nurse, and that's why the dad had to keep him hidden from the world - he was hiding own his adultery, not his son's looks. The mother's dying wish was to curse the family, and Victor's birth mother died immediately after having him.

There is almost a completely new set of characters, since most from the first film were killed. Marybeth is back, but this time played by Danielle Harris. Harris is well-loved by the horror community, many of whom remember her from her first role as Jamie Lloyd in *Halloween 4: The Return of Michael Myers* (Dir. Dwight H. Little, 1988). To explain why Marybeth was recast, Green spoke with Screen Rant in June of 2020:

"The simple answer is that it wasn't gonna work out. I think she was taking some bad advice in handling herself in a bad way with us... We planned *Hatchet II* before we did *Hatchet*. We had this whole storyline planned out and were going to start the movie on the same frame the other one ended on. We were like, "Do we change all of that because this pretty much unknown actress is being difficult right now"? So instead we thought "How do we go upwards and onwards and recast her with somebody the fans are going to be even more excited about?"

...I'm happy to see that in all the reviews that have come out, everybody completely loves her and has embraced her and there hasn't even been mention that the part was recast" (Kennedy, 2020).

Regardless of the reasons behind recasting, Harris does an

excellent job with the role. She plays Marybeth differently than Zaragoza did, but in a way that makes sense in her character's arc. The second film picks up immediately after the first film, and the more time we spend with Marybeth, the more awful trauma she endures. Harris plays her as angrier and more aggressive, which is believable for someone who has gone through what she has. However, I did notice. She drops the bayou accent more often than not, and I don't know if that's an intentional choice. Tony Todd is featured much more heavily in the second film, his role of Reverend Zombie critical to the plot. The story focuses more on the locals rather than tourists. Rev. Zombie is rounding up a group of local hunters to kill Victor Crowley for a hefty reward.

Some of the nastiness in the film comes from the script. The dialogue is similarly nasty to that in the first film - especially Vernon (Colton Dunn), who delivers such lines as, "I'd tap that, but she probably got cobwebs sealing it up." There is also a highly sexualized kill during a sex scene in the woods. There is a hermaphrodite joke, and more ableist language. But much of the writing and jokes have grown out of the edginess present in the first film. Overall, there is less nudity in the second film. The film manages to add in a few naked women at the beginning, when the harbinger character finds the video camera from the first film and starts looking through the footage that women were being tricked into providing a fake TV producer. That scene would be forgivable as an obvious play to increase the film's breast count, but there is a wholly unnecessary part on tape when the so-called producer solicits a fourteen-year-old girl. It's played as a joke when the harbinger sees it and says, "That's not right." That's the kind of edgy humor that made the Millennial Nasty decade what it was, and horror movies are less likely to show that kind of joke now.

The first kill is absolutely disgusting in the best way. The harbinger character has his intestines ripped out, and he is dragged and choked with them. It's a perfect opening kill to set us up for the rest of the gore. But the next kill doesn't come until nearly an hour into the movie. However, it's worth the wait, because the body count is high and when the kills begin, they haven't lost any nastiness from the first film. Later we see a face smashed in with a hatchet, a face chopped off, a curb-stomp that cuts a head in half, and the biggest chainsaw in history that chainsaws two men up the crotch at once. There is a death by boat propeller, where one character has his face spiraled away. And Reverend Zombie dies spectacularly at the end of the film, getting cut in half and having his top half ripped out of his skin. Green hoped to avoid another ratings battle with the MPAA, which had caused him trouble with the first film, and just hoped for the film to be unrated (Collis, 2010). In the end, there was an R rated version with cuts, and an unrated director's cut.

For all its gore and violence, it doesn't have the meanness of the first film. Now that the audience is watching Marybeth's point of view, and we have sympathy for her hardship, the movie has a more emotional tone. It's cathartic at the end when Marybeth smashes Crowley's face into a pulp and then shoots him, leaving us with an ending as abrupt as the first films.

By 2010, horror audiences were starting to hunger for something else, and new trends were on their way in. We were less forgiving of bigotry played as humor, and some fans were looking for quieter plots that scared them more slowly. However, this didn't stop the *Hatchet* franchise, and as of now, there are two more sequels which were released in 2013 and 2017. They always bring a who's who of horror celebrities, and fans of slashers, nastiness, and the franchise will keep showing up for them, as long as they are made. *Hatchet* and *Hatchet II* are great examples of how the torture porn characteristics could be translated into a slasher film and make a Millennial Nasty.

BREAK SOME BONES TO BREAK THE MOLD.

The Millennial Nasty decade was ready to give us something fresh and new and break some rules. *Hatchet* and *Wrong Turn* had crossover appeal to fans of more traditional torture porn, and fans of more traditional slashers. They did alienate some people who missed the glossiness in slashers from the '90s, and *Hatchet* didn't have as much mainstream buzz until years later. But what will forever remain true in a slasher: whether you stay on the path or stray from it, you have to …

# BE CAREFUL WHO YOU MESS WITH

Joy Ride (2001) and Joy Ride 2: Dead Ahead (2008)

## *Joy Ride* (AKA *Road Kill*) 2001

> "I think sometimes people don't know
> what they're doing, you know?"

*Joy Ride*, directed by John Dahl, is a slasher that takes place on a road trip, rather than in a single location. When college student Lewis (Paul Walker) sees an opportunity to help his crush Venna (Leelee Sobieski), he jumps at the opportunity and buys a used car to drive them both home from college. Along the way, he picks up his estranged brother, Fuller (Steve Zahn), who has just been released from jail (not for the first time) after a drunk and disorderly charge. Fuller installs a CB radio while Lewis is distracted and treats it like a new toy. The brothers pretend to be long-haul truck drivers and giggle to themselves while they make connections over the radio.

It's a road trip slasher. The slasher elements begin as the boys play a prank and anger the wrong person. Lewis uses a high voice to sound unconvincingly female and calls himself

Candy Cane, flirting with a trucker called Rusty Nail (voiced terrifyingly by Ted Levine). When Rusty Nail realizes Candy Cane is a fictional character voiced by a man, he kills a stranger in a fit of rage and hunts down the brothers. One of the tensest scenes in the film takes place as Fuller and Lewis are listening through the thin motel wall, and it sounds like there is a violent fight between Rusty Nail and the other lodger. The audience isn't shown anything other than Lewis and Fuller listening intently, becoming more and more unsettled. The focus is on the painting on the motel room wall, a scene of a stormy night at sea, signaling the calm before the storm for the boys. This scene is lit in the sickly yellow-green so popular for horror films at the time, and this scene marks the turning point from silly road-trip comedy into a horror film. From this point in the film, Rusty Nail is pursuing the road trippers and demanding an apology.

Smart filmmaking decisions are what make this movie scary, because it's hard to have empathy for the characters' choices. We barely ever see Rusty Nail, and he remains a mysterious figure, willing to kill because of his embarrassment and demanding an apology. Instead, his truck is positioned as the monster visible of the film. It's huge, and it can both slink through the darkness and burst onto the scene, like any of our favorite slasher killers. The exhaust stacks appear to be breathing, and the headlights move to look around like eyes. During a terrifying scene in a cornfield, the truck almost seems to be alive, tracking and chasing prey like an apex predator.

There is another tense scene in which the brothers think they are being chased by Rusty Nail in his truck, but it turns out to be another innocent trucker, returning a credit card Lewis left behind at a gas station. As the brothers and the audience are coming down from the red herring scare, Rusty Nail's truck crashes through the smaller truck, smashing it in half, absolutely destroying it, like Jason Voorhees bursting through a window.

The film's position in history is interesting, especially during this time period. It was released near the beginning of the Millennial Nasty decade, and while it's not the nastiest film in this book, it relies on some dark themes and brutal kills, choosing what to show and what to keep off screen. Perhaps if it had come later in the decade, more violence would have been on screen. It was created pre-9/11, and released just after, on October 5th, 2001. If 9/11 marked a turning point in what audiences wanted in their entertainment, especially horror, this film whets their appetites for nastier films to come later. It shows its age, as a car is purchased with a refundable airline ticket printed on paper. Paper tickets are a thing of the past, and the idea of a refundable airline ticket that a college student could afford seems absurd now. Fuller calls the CB radio "prehistoric internet," which makes me chuckle, as their understanding of the internet and its capabilities in 2001 seems "prehistoric" now.

The assumptions made by the plot and characters shape the themes of *Joy Ride* and place the film in the Millennial Nasty category. Male egos drive the plot. Toxic masculinity, gender expectations, and homophobia play important parts in the story. Fuller is punching his brother and encouraging him to take part in so-called pranks that lead to Rusty Nail's embarrassment, and ultimately, violence. Lewis doesn't really want to be involved, but Fuller convinces him through cajoling and chiding. Fuller confronts Lewis about his relationship to Venna, aggressively asking if he's "fucking her." Fuller also says later in the film, after the scare with the truck driver returning Lewis's wallet, "I've never felt like more a pussy in my whole life," and of course the use of the word "pussy" equates femininity with weakness and fear. Candy Cane only exists as a sex joke, which hurts Rusty Nail's ego. He demands an apology, but Fuller insists they will not apologize, indulging his own big ego. If the men in this film would have respected each other more, and not been so afraid of appearing weak, none of the violence would have happened.

The treatment of women in this film is ripe for discussion. Venna is the female character who gets the most screen time. Her character doesn't have much agency or personality, she seems to exist for the male characters to react to. She passively agrees to Lewis picking her up from school. She acts however the guys want her to act, in one scene advocating for following rules and acting sensibly, and in the next, taking shots at the bar and flirting. When they stop for drinks on the road, Fuller pushes his way into her motel room, while Lewis is already passed out. Venna doesn't say no, but she also doesn't say yes, and Fuller comes in to make them drinks. It's framed as charming, and the movie thinks it is charming, instead of alarming. He is insisting they continue drinking, and it's implied he wants to sleep with her. This is predatory behavior. The guys don't initially tell Venna they are being pursued by a stranger they anger and teased. They keep her uninformed in an unsafe situation because it would be inconvenient to tell her the truth. Venna is more willing than the guys to follow the instructions given by Rusty Nail. Most likely, Venna has no agency because she is a plot device. But the film, perhaps accidentally, provides commentary on the way women are socialized to appease men to survive and stay safe. Many women are taught to politely go with the flow so they can get through, if not unscathed, at least alive. The other woman we meet in this film, albeit briefly, is Venna's roommate, Charlotte (Jessica Bowman), who is sweet and feminine. She exists only as a character for Rusty Nail to kill as the tension builds for the main characters.

Not only do all the male characters get more screen time and development, but the portrayal of masculinity is starkly different from that of femininity. When they are at the roadside bar, some men start calling Venna a bitch and Lewis "college boy," and turn their harassment on the brothers when they stand up for Venna. Fuller gets them out of the tense situation by talking like the men who are harassing them, matching their regional accent, calling Venna his bitch and telling her to behave, and rushing the group out of the bar. While the film portrays that blatant harassment of women shouldn't be tolerated, it also suggests that women need saving by men, and that the best way to do that is not to stand up for the women, but to remove them from the situation. Sometimes, in real life, it is best to do what's safest. But they could have just left the bar, instead of Fuller tacitly condoning their behavior and language. Even the fictional woman, Candy Cane, only exists to amuse men, and ceases to exist when she becomes trouble. In *Joy Ride*, women are not active participants, things just happen to them at the hands of men.

On the *Horror Queers podcast*, the hosts Joe Lipsett and Trace Thurman discuss gay panic in their *Joy Ride* episode (October 2021), and they cite Eric Langber's article "Outside Of Laramie: Joy Ride (2001) As Gay Panic Horror" from Gayly Dreadful in 2020. The discussion explores how much *Joy Ride* relies on Rusty Nail being angry that he was flirting with a man, not a woman. It's clear that if Candy Cane had been a real woman who was just leading him on, he would have been furious, but he probably wouldn't have tracked her down and killed her. Straight men having their sexuality challenged was enough of a plot for a horror film because, at this time, there was still a lot of public disgust for queerness. On *Horror Queers*, they point out that one of the stops on the road trip is Laramie, Wyoming. Laramie is best known for the tragic and horrific murder of Matthew Shepard, a young gay man who was killed in one of the most notorious homophobic hate crimes in America's history. I can't say for sure if this was a purposeful nod by the filmmakers, or if it is pure coincidence, but knowing the facts, I cannot think about *Joy Ride* without acknowledging how much violence gay panic has caused.

There are also, likely accidentally, many points made about class and privilege. The three main characters, especially the brothers, do not consider the consequences of their actions. We don't know much about the background of our main characters, but two of them are lucky enough to be going to colleges out of their home state, which is usually more expensive than in-state tuition. While Fuller has been in and out of jail, it's clear that the system keeps giving him chances, which might mean he has enough money to pay fines and move on. If he can bail himself out of jail for minor offenses, he's less motivated to examine the consequence of his actions. All three of the main cast are white, and likely unaware of their white privilege. They don't need to be as afraid as people of color when they have confrontations with the law. The main characters do not see the police as a threat, and in fact, see the police as helpful. This attitude toward police was certainly common in media at the time, and especially after 9/11. But even in this story written pre 9/11, and one of the main characters having had many run-ins with the law, they see police as allies. Similarly, people see Lewis and Fuller as non-threatening, likely due in part to their class and race. At one point in the film, Rusty Nail demands they embarrass themselves to pay for his embarrassment. He instructs them to walk naked into a diner in the middle of the day and order food at the counter. This is presented as a tense joke, and the diner customers look on in horror, and cover their children's eyes. But no one yells at them or threatens to call the police. Grown men naked in public would most likely be considered a threat and is definitely illegal. But the men in the movie call it an embarrassment, and the movie itself presents it as a joke. Lewis and Fuller are scared of Rusty Nail, but there is no acknowledgment of greater consequences from society for being naked in public.

Even within white America, the brothers draw a line between themselves and Rusty Nail, treating him as an Other. Lewis and Fuller begin their entertainment on the CB radio by imitating southern-American accents and using the lingo of truckers. They don't say it outright, but they view truck drivers as less than themselves. They assume the truckers are too stupid to pick up on the fact that the boys are playing around, even though it's painfully obvious. They want to put on the costume and play Trucker, and then take the costume off when it stops being fun. That's something people with privilege don't always understand that they are doing and why it can be harmful. They want what they assume are the fun and funny parts of being a truck driver, but they ignore the parts they think are below them, like the actual job of driving a truck.

The brothers and the film explicitly draw a line in the sand at racism. They are willing to be classist and sexist, even without meaning to, but they feel disgusted when they witness overt racist comments. They stop at a motel, and another guest says hateful and racist things to the person working at the reception desk. They decide to prank both this racist person and Rusty Nail by sending Rusty Nail to his room for sex. That's a bad idea because it gets the other guest killed, and sets Rusty Nail on a path of revenge, but it's also a thoughtless approach to how to solve problems in the world. Lewis and Fuller are satisfied with pranking one racist person and moving on. It makes them feel like they did something to address racism, when really they solved nothing. What's worse, they do not consider the fallout that could come (especially to non-white people) from their actions.

This is a story about actions and their consequences. Should Lewis and Fuller be hunted down and killed for playing a thoughtless, harmful joke? No. And Rusty Nail shouldn't be murdering people. But the fact that the brothers don't even think about the possibility of consequences, combined with the social commentary presented by this film, makes a unique slasher, and more thoughtful than it seems at first glance. A sentiment from Fuller foreshadows the bleakness that would dominate horror for the rest of the decade. After their motel neighbor is murdered, Lewis asks him "how he can just drive away from this," and Fuller responds, "Just remind yourself that in 100 years you're gonna be dead. That's the closest thing I've got to a philosophy." What a dark way to unburden yourself of the consequences of your choices.

## *Joy Ride 2: Dead Ahead* (2008)

"Everything's dead here."

The direct-to-video sequel, directed by Louis Morneau, follows a more traditional slasher formula, but still has similar themes to the first film. But first, a nasty slasher opening, complete with sex and violence. It's a dark rainy night at a truck stop, and a sex worker climbs into the cab of a long-haul truck. We still don't see Rusty Nail's face, but we hear his gravelly voice (although not provided by Ted Levine this time). He tells the sex worker to expose her breasts and remove her wig, before killing her for seemingly no reason. It serves as a great cold-open for a slasher, and it immediately lets the audience know this movie is going to be different from its predecessor. In the first film, Rusty Nail only killed those who embarrassed him and got in his way, as far as we can tell. Now, he seems like he kills just because. Maybe he got a taste for it after the murders in the first film, but in any case, Rusty Nail (Mark Gibbon) is a different kind of monster this time around.

In this film, we again follow a group of young people who are on a road trip, this time to Las Vegas for a wedding. Melissa (Nicki Aycox) and Bobby (Nick Zano) are getting married, and Melissa's sister Kayla (Laura Jordan) is coming along for support. They pick up Kayla's relatively new boyfriend, Nik (Kyle Schmid), and the four are on their way. Melissa is the Final Girl, as evidenced by her relationships and tendency to follow the rules. Her relationship with Bobby seems sweet enough, and she loves her trouble-making sister, much like Lewis loved Fuller despite his flaws. Nik fills a role that wasn't in the first film, as a sexy, loudmouth counterpart to the slightly wild sister. Nik is rude and objectionable the whole time, but for some reason the group takes his idea to follow back roads across the county, when he insists it will be a more interesting trip. The car breaks down almost immediately, because

Melissa's car runs out of oil. Audiences can question the decisions so far: why drive, rather than fly; if driving, why not take better care of your car; and if you know you don't take care of your car, why leave the main roads? But it's a slasher setup, and it's what we signed up for.

While looking for help, they come upon an empty house, and it's reminiscent of *The Texas Chain Saw Massacre* (1974). The house is not abandoned, but they let themselves in, looking for a phone. As in many slashers, young people have little regard for how their actions might be perceived by others, and just take the world as their own. They decide to steal a beautiful Chevelle - complete with a CB radio, of course - that's covered in the garage, and they leave a note that they will bring the car back. This is the most unrealistic decision in the film - even if we accept that wild-guy Nik might suggest stealing a car, there is no way we believe Melissa would go along with it. But she does. Well, it turns out, they robbed Rusty Nail, who lives in a lovely country home. He pursues them, kills them one by one and plays mind games with them, in an amplified version of what we saw in the first film.

While much of this film is reminiscent of the slick-looking '90s slashers, the darkness in the story and the violence put it snugly in the Millennial Nasty category. Rusty Nail is much more brutal, and his actions are darker and meaner. For example, he demands Kayla cut off finger, as a punishment for the group. But they send him a finger stolen from a dead body in a random morgue, and when Rusty Nail realizes this, he is more furious than before. As punishment for trying to trick him, he orders Melissa to strip down to her underwear while he watches from his truck. Melissa, being the pure Final Girl that she is, is visibly horrified but willing to protect her friends. However, Rusty Nail adds another layer of cruelty. He has sent a stranger in another truck to watch Melissa, who then propositions her for sex. Melissa is humiliated and horrified, and Rusty Nail laughs at her over the CB radio. The movie presents this as bad behavior from Rusty Nail, which is a step up from the jokey naked-in-the-diner scene in the first film. But at the time, sexual assault and harassment still had a long way to go in terms of public understanding, and the movie doesn't realize how traumatic this scene would be for Melissa.

This film has a much more explicit exploration of gender and class than the first one, though its point is unclear. It touches on issues of class because Nik is excessively vocal about his hate of truck drivers. He loudly talks badly about truckers in a truck stop diner and takes any opportunity he can to put them down. It's later revealed that his father was a trucker, and he harbors resentment toward his father. However, the only purpose of this plot point seems to be to make Nik an unlikable character, and to pit him against truck drivers in general. It doesn't amount to much in the plot. The scene with the most to unpack regarding gender and sexuality is a scene where Nik is forced to dress as a woman and buy crystal methamphetamine. Rusty Nail sets him on this task, knowing it might get him killed. The language throughout the scene ranges from neutral ("we're gonna make sure you pass as a girl") to downright transphobic (use of the word "tranny"). Rusty Nail threatens to cut off Nik's penis to "complete his transformation." It's framed as a horror that Nik is forced to wear a skirt, wig, makeup, and high heels, and walk through a truck stop party looking for illicit drugs. Nik is more afraid of dressing like a woman than he is of going to buy meth. His masculinity is so fragile that he can't stand acting like a woman for a short time for his own survival. While it may not have been the goal of the filmmakers, the film certainly presents that one of the worst things that can happen is a man being forced into a dress, even worse than what Melissa went through, being coerced into sexual acts for survival. And the film is certainly not coming at it from a positive direction, although I suppose you could read it that way: being forced to act like a gender that you're not is traumatic. Read that way, it's trans-positive, but that's not how the scene is presented. During a torture scene later (the best scene in the film, in my opinion), Nik is still wearing the dress and wig. Bobby and Nik are tied to chairs across from each other at a table, and Rusty Nail is rolling dice to decide what kind of torture to inflict. The torture game setup must be a nod to the *Saw* franchise, which was booming at the time. Bobby hangs by a chain around his neck, and Nik is branded with an R made out of nails heated with a blowtorch. Rusty Nail replaces Nik's wig back on his head before killing him with rebar through the head. Why replace the wig? Does Rusty Nail prefer to hurt women, or queer people, or people he perceives as queer? Homophobia certainly sent him over the edge in the first film. Rusty Nail's motivation is not obvious, but the fact that he replaces Nik's wig before penetrating him to death is impossible to ignore.

In *Joy Ride 2*, Rusty Nail reminds me of Mick, the killer in the *Wolf Creek* films. Like Mick, he traps people at his home and tortures them, for minor perceived slights. Rusty Nail is a monster, and the truck and radio are his weapons. He initially starts chasing the group of friends because they took his Chevelle, but in the end, he smashes that car anyway.

Rusty Nail should die in an explosive truck crash at the end of the film, and at first, we assume that's what happened. But the film ends with a young woman getting in a truck cab, and we see the truck driver's burned arm and hear his gravelly laugh. Somehow, Rusty Nail survived for a third and final film in 2014, *Joy Ride 3: Road Kill*, and while it left the door open for other sequels, the horror landscape had changed so much by then, no one was looking for a fourth *Joy Ride* film.

> **"Now they know what it feels like... to be the butt-end of the joke."**
>
> — RUSTY NAIL

The first two *Joy Ride* films are Millennial Nasties and slashers because of their stalk-and-kill formulas, their dark implications and themes, and the brutal violence of the time. Especially post 9/11, America was looking to hold terrorists accountable for their actions, and driving home the message that actions had consequences was something that rang true for audiences. Framing that message with ignorant young people who made the wrong choices made for interesting stories, and the nasty films we craved. But whether or not we make the right choices, even if we mess up and apologize, we must remember...

# YOU CAN'T CHEAT DEATH
## THE FINAL DESTINATION FRANCHISE

FINAL DESTINATION (2000), FINAL DESTINATION 2 (2003), FINAL DESTINATION 3 (2006), AND THE FINAL DESTINATION (2009)

The *Final Destination* franchise is the second-most important franchise of this era, second only to *Saw*. *Final Destination* spans nearly the whole decade, from the year 2000 through 2009. Similar to *Saw*, it both sets the tone for the era, and is in conversation with it, as it continues to ramp up on its gore and nastiness as the years go by.

There has been much conversation over the years about which subgenre the *Final Destination* films fit into. They have qualities of both the '90s glossy slashers, like *Scream* (Wes Craven, 1996) and *I Know What You Did Last Summer* (Jim Gillespie, 1997) (and their sequels). But they have the dark themes and splattery kills of a torture porn film. I almost never hear them get included in the torture porn conversation with the *Saw* and *Hostel* franchises. They have more in common with a slasher, following the formula of a group of frightened (usually young) people trying to figure out what's happening while they die one by one. But there is no masked stalker, no who-done-it plotline. The killer in the *Final Destination* films is Death itself. The franchise stares in the face of the truth everyone has to face every day: that we are all going to die one day, and we may be able to prolong our lives, if we're lucky, but there is no true escape from Death. The joyful way these films play with this bleak topic bring them into Millennial Nasty territory.

The deaths in the *Final Destination* films are brutal, and while the gore varies from film to film, they are all devastating deaths. Each film begins with a protagonist having a vision of a group of people dying in an accident - for example, in the first film, a plane crash. The person who has the vision encourages everyone to safety and saves a handful of people who follow their lead. But as they learn, "Death has a design," and if they were supposed to die in an accident, Death is coming for them one by one, picking off stragglers who got away. Most of the films in the franchise wisely mix practical and digital effects to create scenes that are still impactful today (the outlier being the fourth one, shot in 3D, but we will get to that). In every sequel, the mechanics of the deaths become more and more elaborate, and the kills less predictable. The Domino effects of the deaths are not unlike the way the killer operates in *The Collector* (2009) (but this is maybe the only time you will hear those film franchises compared to one another).

What sets apart *Final Destinatio*n from some of the other Millennial Nasties is the polished feel of the films, the big names attached to the cast, and the way the films lean into self-parody rather than doubling down on taking themselves more seriously. Each film follows a similar template. Often, new rules or lore are added. The execution of the formula is more than enough to keep us coming back for more. A unique trait of this franchise, established in the first film and mostly carried throughout, is the way it sits with grief after character deaths. Often in slashers, either the surviving characters are focused on escaping a killer, or they don't yet know their friends are dead, or both, and so there isn't much of a focus on grief. In the *Final Destination* franchise, we see the characters going to funerals, reading eulogies, looking through photographs and crying. The impacts of the deaths are felt in these films.

Part of the fun of these films is the way they invite the audience to interact. Each film has clues about Death's design, and fans of the franchise were rewarded for paying attention. For example, the flight number of the plane that crashes in the first film is Flight 180, as in, "you should turn around 180 degrees and walk away from this." Several of the films have "death songs," tunes that play to warn the characters and the audience that Death's design is in motion. The first film built a successful franchise that's still loved today.

### *Final Destination* (2000)

"You can't cheat death."

James Wong's *Final Destination* follows the story of Alex (Devon Sawa) and a group of his friends who were on their way to France for a school trip. Alex has a vision of the plane exploding, and a group of students are forced off, including Alex's best friend Tod (Chad Donella). Also present is quirky, quiet Clear, played by Ali Larter. The plane does explode, and the surviving kids who had exited the plane begin dying in the order they would have died in the place explosion. The famous Tony Todd plays a character called Bludworth, or as I like to call him, the exposition mortician (he works in the morgue and explains important plot points!). When Alex and his friends talk with Bludworth, the kids realize that the survivors are dying in the order they would have in the plane explosion. They discover that they can continue to save one another, sending Death down the line to circle back on the remaining survivors.

The kills in this film take their time. Tension builds while the characters and the audience are waiting to see what will happen next, and how the next person will die. Tod's death is the first to truly display Death's design. Tod slips on water from a leaky toilet, and falls into the shower, where he can't get his footing on spilled shampoo. A clothesline wire wraps around his neck, and it looks like he hung himself in the shower. His loved ones accept that idea, since Tod had been grieving. The teacher who got off the plane with the students, Ms. Lewton (Kristen Cloke), has an equally tense build up to her death, especially now that the audience can see it coming. A cracked mug drips vodka into her computer, which explodes and sends shrapnel into her neck. Her kitchen catches fire, and while trying to put it out, a knife falls into her chest. Since it's the first film, the audience was learning the rules along with the characters, and the story takes its time to reveal its structure.

The timing of this film is important. It was completely created and released well before the 9/11 terrorist attacks. It was released in the U.S. on March 17th, 2000, about a year and a half before 9/11 took place. And it's obvious, in the filmmaking. The way the characters freely move about the airport, and the things they are allowed to bring on an international flight, those pieces of the past are gone forever. This movie could not have been made after 9/11, at least, not for a long time, and then it might not have been the right time. Or possibly, it could have been made with an accident other than a plane explosion. After 9/11, the world, but especially America, was not ready to see mass transit accidents in film, especially happening to innocent, predominantly white American teenagers. Every subsequent film in the franchise was released after 9/11, but audiences were already comfortable enough with the *Final Destination* story to keep coming back.

The first film seems like it's going to have a happy ending, with three survivors going to Paris for the vacation they never got to take. There is an abrupt, darkly comedic ending when a character unexpectedly dies, and the movie simply ends. The abrupt finality of that moment emphasized the fact that there really is no cheating Death. The surprising ending and the open-ended story left audiences hungry for more, which we were lucky enough to receive.

## *Final Destination 2* (2003)

> "People are always most alive just before
> they die."

Directed by David R. Ellis, the second film begins on the one-year anniversary of the events of the first movie. Kimberly (A.J. Cook) is going on a road trip with her friends, but she has a premonition of a horrible pile up on the highway. She manages to save herself, and a few strangers, but her friends don't make it. Surrounded by news coverage of the one-year anniversary, Kimberly realizes what's happening.

She goes to Clear for help, the only surviving character from the first film. Clear has checked herself into a mental hospital and spends her days in a white padded cell to keep herself safe from Death's designs. Clear is reluctant to leave, and give up her safety, but Kimberly convinces her they need Clear's help. Kimberly experiences visions that help her guess how the next person will die, but she never puts the pieces together in time to save anyone. Her visions are never explained. They are just an accepted part of the plot to move the story forward, which makes the second film a little less serious than the first. But the plot already hinges on the supernatural, and adding a character with recurring premonitions doesn't hurt the experience of watching the story unfold. The twist in this film is that the group of characters were all somehow involved in the plane accident from the first film. Either they could have been on the plane or cleaning up the accident. The second film is Death tying up loose ends from Flight 180.

This film adds to the lore of the first. This time, if one character saves another's life, that Good Samaritan will be killed next. Thinking critically, that could send the message of "never save someone's life," but it's unlikely that the makers of *Final Destination 2* wanted anyone to take away that lesson. Another piece of lore introduced is that new life can cancel out death. At first, it seems like a newborn baby will break the cycle. One of the characters saved from the opening car crash is pregnant, and the survivors assume when she gives birth, they will all be safe. They realize that isn't true, and what "new life" means is reviving a survivor who was killed. A new baby does seem to pause Death's design, but as the first film taught us, you can't cheat Death.

This film impacted an entire generation of drivers. Ask anyone who has seen this film how they feel driving behind a log truck on the highway. *Final Destination 2* took something so mundane, so everyday, and made it horrifying. The plane crash in the first one is scary, of course, but most people do not get on a plane every day. Many people, however, especially in the Western Hemisphere, do drive on the highway every day. Especially in the U.S., which is huge, and because resources have to travel far from one place to another, log trucks are a common occurrence. The simplicity of terror in that sequence lives on in the back of many of our minds.

### *Final Destination 3* (2006)

> "You can run, but you cannot hide. This is
>      the beginning of the end."

By the time audiences experienced *Final Destination 3*, we knew what we were in for, and we were ready to have fun with it. James Wong returned to direct and made the most beloved sequel of the franchise. The characters are loveable, the deaths are more brutal than ever, and there is a perfect mix of sincerity and self-awareness for the third film in the franchise. While we don't see Bludworth in this film, we do get a voiceover from

Tony Todd. By now, audiences knew most of the characters would not make it out alive, and we just wanted to be along for the ride. Fittingly, this film opens with a ride: a rollercoaster. The film follows a group of teens, as usual, and begins with them at a school carnival night. The premonition and first tragedy take place are based on a rollercoaster accident.

The most iconic death sequence in this film is in a tanning salon. Tanning was widely recognized to be dangerous in 2006, but it was still a popular beauty trend, especially for white teenage girls. In *Final Destination 3*, tanning turned out to be more dangerous than we were warned. The characters Ashley (Chelan Simmons) and Ashlyn (Yan-Kay Crystal Lowe) are burned alive, trapped in their tanning beds, and it is nasty. A series of small accidents keeps the salon owner trapped outside, unable to help, while a shelf locks the girls into the tanning beds. They are screaming and crying, trying to force their way out. Meanwhile, their skin is blistering and melting. These two characters are interesting. They are presented as vapid airheads, but they are not mean. They seem self-obsessed, but we don't see them harming others. In a slasher, you might expect the sexy high school girls to be cruel, but these two are not. They are best friends, and they enjoy each other. It makes their death heartbreaking, especially with how grotesque it is. It's also worth mentioning this is the first time - and one of the only times - the franchise has any nudity. We see their breasts before they die, but it doesn't seem gratuitous. They are best friends tanning together; it makes sense they would be topless and comfortable around each other. There were other horror films to feature tanning bed deaths or near-deaths, but none nearly as memorable. The camera focusing on their boiling skin without shying away, while they screamed, and "Love Rollercoaster" by the Ohio Players played in the background makes this tanning bed death take the top spot.

This film walks a fine line between horror and comedy. A character that places this movie firmly in its time is Frankie

Cheeks (Sam Easton), a sexual predator whose behavior is presented as a joke. He's taking upskirt photos (obviously without consent) and making lewd comments to every girl he sees. The previous films hadn't had a character like this, and the addition for Cheeks is likely due to the timing, with raunchy comedies being at the height of popularity, and the way the third film leans into some silliness. It's much less likely to see a film made today that would play Frankie Cheeks as a comedic character. However, that irreverence is juxtaposed with grief in this film. We sit with grief even more in this film than in the previous two, watching the impact on families and friends, visiting graveyards over the shoulders of the main characters. Instead of being just a race away from death, we contemplate it. It makes the characters even more loveable, and their deaths that much more tragic.

The third film tends to be a fan favorite, because it feels like the franchise really hit its stride and knew what would please the audience. Less time is spent on exposition, and there is a greater focus on the deaths. The next film didn't quite land the same way for fans.

### *The Final Destination* (AKA *Final Destination 4*) (2009)

> "What if us being here right now was the
> plan from the beginning?"

In 2009, the years of nasty violence were starting to become a little stale, and many of the films near the end of the era were simply churning out gore to make money. That means this film, though directed by the director of the second *Final Destination* film and *Snakes on a Plane* (2006), David R. Ellis, was going through the motions and applying the formula, without adding anything interesting. It was released just one year before *SAW 3D* and was also shot in 3D. It suffers the same problem years later, and it looks substandard on modern high-definition TVs.

It relied heavily on CGI, which is in stark contrast to the love the previous films showed for practical effects.

Another similarity to *Saw 3D* is the use of a racist character. It's interesting that racism was recognized, portrayed, but then simply solved by killing the racist. Similar action occurred in *Joy Ride* (2001). This plot point of swiftly dispatching one racist person clearly portrays the confusion America felt at the time, trying to grapple with racial injustice. Many Americans considered racism solved in the '90s, and now were struggling with how untrue that was. But instead of trying to understand and work through what it means to have systemically racist structures, we wanted to cheer when the racist person was killed onscreen. That could push the guilt away, if only for a little while (and only if you were white).

One theme briefly explored in this film is watching violence and tragedy for entertainment. The first accident takes place at a stock car race, when a horrible crash causes part of the stands to collapse and kill spectators. Before the crash, the main characters are talking about hoping to see a car wreck and saying that's the only reason to attend this kind of event. That's absolutely a stereotype of people who enjoy stock car racing, that they only want to see a crash. But that conversion covertly implicates the viewer. If we are judging the characters for wanting to see a crash, aren't we the same? Don't we come to a *Final Destination* film for the kills? Of course, there is a difference between wishing to see real-life tragedy and violence and wanting to see it onscreen in fictional stories. But for a crash-grab movie, it makes a wise point for us to consider. Where is the line when you are wishing to see violence?

Meant to be the final film in the franchise, it spends no time on exposition, and doesn't add any new rules for the characters to discover or navigate. However, it does add one piece of information, right at the end. The characters realize, right before they die, that this was Death's plan all along. They were supposed to survive up until this point, and know they are right where

Death wants them. If this is true, it means the actions of everyone in the previous films didn't make any difference to their survival. It's a darkly poignant ending to an otherwise fun franchise.

**"There are no escapes."**

— BLUDWORTH

Because humans will never stop struggling with the idea of death, and trying to survive, the *Final Destination* films will always be relevant, and horror fans will stay hungry for more. A fifth film was released in 2011, and as I type this sentence, a sixth film is in the works. Hopefully, the early-aughts homophobia and other assorted bigotry will be missing, but I can't wait to see Death's new design. Look past the glossy slasher and the teen romance, and the entire *Final Destination* franchise is an examination of existential dread. Most people try to live as long as we can, though we know in the end, Death is coming for us, one way or another.

# PART THREE

---

THE ERA OF REMAKES

# NASTI-FICATION FOR A NEW GENERATION

## THE REMAKE SURGE

Filmmakers and film studios realized they could cash in on horror fandom by pumping out tons of remakes in the 2000s. Some horror fans loved this and saw it as a chance to revisit old favorites in a new way. And some (very vocal) horror fans hated it, and felt that it tainted the originals, and wanted people to just go watch the original classics. Those who hated these movies loved to hate them, and remakes were on every horror fan's mind.

Most of the horror being remade at the time was from the '70s and '80s. Enough time had passed for the stories to be ready for a refresh, but not so long they had fallen out of style with fans. Many of the folk and slasher horror films of the '70s and '80s were reactions to violence and war in the world at the time, and much of the world was at war again in the 2000s, and fear of The Other was prevalent enough again in America to make that the crux of a scary story.

Most of the remakes added backstory to their villains and sometimes added explanations that were meant to garner sympathy from viewers. This was divisive among audiences.

Some horror fans believed the killers were more frightening when we didn't have an explanation for their behavior, and that backstory watered down the killers' images. But some fans enjoyed the additions, offering something creative to a familiar story.

Love them or hate them, there are plenty of remakes to watch, and these remakes leaned into the style of the time to offer unique takes on familiar stories. Have another look with me.

# PUNISH THE BITCHES

Horror stories have not always been kind to women. In the Millennial Nasty era, there are examples of women in horror films being treated terribly by the story. Two slasher remakes in particular display a meanness toward women that cannot be ignored. *Black Christmas* and *Sorority Row* are remakes of slashers that were special in their own time. The original *Black Christmas* (Dir. Bob Clark, 1974) may be the first movie to establish the modern slasher template. These two remakes, while they offer a lot to love, got lost among the other remakes and nasty films of the time. I believe that's because the original *Black Christmas* is so well-loved, fans were hesitant about a remake, and *The House on Sorority Row* (Dir. Mark Rosman, 1982) is relatively obscure, so it didn't have name recognition with fans. These are opposite sides of the same problem.

The 2000s were a time of pushing boundaries in film, especially in horror. Both films discussed in this chapter balance horror and comedy, flavored by the edginess and raunchiness of the time. The goal at the time was to push buttons - the misguided idea that if you offended everyone, you were treating people equally. We were post second-wave feminism and into the third wave, wherein women were taking back their sexuality and proudly reveling in their femininity. However, women were still expected to meet certain societal expectations, and films were still often driven by the male gaze. Women were encouraged to insult and scoff at feminism while still caring about voting and reproductive rights. We weren't supposed to call ourselves feminists, but we were expected to encompass feminist values on our own time. We made fun of ourselves, and jokes at our expense were ok. Women were supposed to be satisfied with the power we had and move on. We were expected to "take a joke," even if it was mean, and laugh along with the internalized misogyny disguising itself as feminism. That meant, in the 2000s, there was a free pass to be openly mean to women on film.

Two films encompass all these contrasting, confusing messages perfectly, and do it in the slasher format, with well-made and well-cast films that are fun to watch. Both films take place in sorority houses and involve the sorority sisters, offering plenty of chances to explore the portrayal of women.

### *Black Christmas* (2006)

> "I'd like to bury the hatchet with my
> sister…right in her head."

Because the original is so beloved, any remake was going to have an uphill battle. Glen Morgan's 2006 remake, sometimes called *Black Xmas*, is a vastly different film from the original, to say the least. They both use the same setup of sorority sisters receiving threatening phone calls before Christmas break and being picked off one by one. In the original, the twist is that "the calls are coming from inside the house," and the remake creatively pulls that off in the era of cells phones and caller ID. It's not only a remake - it's one of the earliest examples of a recent trend: the "requel," a film that both acts as a remake of the original while building on the original story. In the 2006 film, the sorority house used to be the house of the killer, who gets a name and a backstory in this film. Many fans of the original were annoyed by this, because one of the things that makes the original so frightening is how little we understand about the killer and his motivation. The remake uses relationship drama to add a red herring possible killer, but it's a far cry from the original feminist storyline of Jess (Olivia Hussey) telling Peter (Keir Dullea) she's getting an abortion.

*Black Xmas* balances on a fine edge of being a beautiful, wintry, Christmassy movie, and being nasty. Every scene is awash in Christmas lights, the spirit of the season is frequently mentioned, and exchanging gifts spurs many plot points. A fun Easter egg (Christmas present?) for fans, Phyl (Andrea Martin) from the original plays the housemother in the 2006 film. She watches over a group of sorority sisters, who are preparing for their various winter break plans. Every year, they do a secret Santa gift exchange, and someone always has to buy a present for Billy Lenz (Robert Mann), who is now a convicted killer. Billy grew up in the house and snapped one Christmas and killed his family. In the original, the killer is never actually named, but it's implied his name is Billy. In the remake, we see some of Billy's childhood, and those scenes are lit in green and yellow, making them sickly and unpleasant. His mother hates him and keeps him locked in the attic. The nastiest point in the plot is that she rapes her pre-teen son, and becomes pregnant with a daughter, Agnes (Dean Friss) (a similar trauma experienced by the killers in *Captivity*). The rape is not shown, which was a wise decision, because the implication is nasty enough. As an adult, Billy is locked up in Clark sanitarium (of course a nod to Bob Clark, the director of the original), and it's a well-known fact he tries to escape every Christmas. This year, he succeeds, and makes his way home. Unfortunately, there's a bad snowstorm, making it hard for the sisters to escape when the killings start. The kills are standard for slashers of the time - nothing overly gruesome, but enough to feed the appetites of the era. Eyes are removed and eaten, and perhaps the grossest flashback is when Billy beats his mother to death and makes cookies from the skin off her back, dipping them in milk before chewing them slowly. A couple of the kills pay homage to the original - there is a plastic bag over the head of a girl sitting in a rocking chair, and there is a stabbing with a crystal unicorn.

The original *Black Christmas* might be the first slasher, or at least one of the first to set the template going forward. It was made before such a template existed, so it didn't have any tropes it had to stick to. The themes are feminist in the original - women standing up for themselves, pursuing relationships and sex on their terms, and of course, Jess's choice to have an abortion. While the 2006 remake tells the story differently, it still has feminist themes, but they are more subtle. Not every sorority sister is friends with one another, but the friendships we see are sweet, and they know each other well and care for one another. As in the original, the women in the remake will take care of their sisters in need. The main protagonist, Kelli (Katie Cassidy), learns that her boyfriend has not only been cheating on her, but creating and keeping recordings of their sex without any woman's consent. Of course, Kelli is sad she was cheated on, but she decides to dump her boyfriend and prioritize herself, rather than forgive him and take him back, and that's a feminist message.

I've mentioned some of the nastiness that places this film firmly in the mid-aughts, and it tried to be as edgy as possible without losing the slasher aesthetic. It has a glossy slasher production, popularized by *Scream*, combined with a horrible story, for an interesting intersection as torture porn was taking over and slashers were getting worn out. Unlikable characters were written so audiences would cheer for their deaths. Even though the sorority sisters are friends, they are mean to one another, in a way that's not realistic - no friend group calls each other bitches as much as this movie would have you believe. The hope was that if the audience found them unpleasant, their deaths would be celebrated. Whether or not that's true, it's a dark way to approach your characters. There's little nudity, but there is a lot of sex and sexiness throughout. If the kills had been gorier, the film may have lost the slasher atmosphere it was hoping for.

Near the end of the film, it's revealed that Agnes also grew up and escaped her living situation, teaming up with Billy for Christmas killings. A male actor is used to play adult Agnes. This has been done in films for decades, and it hasn't stopped, when the filmmakers want the woman in question to be more shocking and grotesque. While I doubt it was the intent, casting a man to play a grotesque woman can imply some negative things about trans-women and trans-femme people. The nasty dialogue, the violence, and the dark themes earned this film its place in this chapter.

The pro-woman, pro-sisterhood themes clash with other elements of the film. For one, the misogynistic language thrown around, while typical in this time period, is not a great example of how anyone should talk to or about women. Also, the villain of the movie is Billy's mother. Of course, abusive mothers exist in the real world. But she does the most deplorable things in the film, and while it's not an excuse for Billy's killings, it's easy to see why he ended up a broken person coming out of that home. The sins of the mother echo through time to relatively innocent sorority sisters in the future.

### *Sorority Row* (2009)

"Cheers, slut."

*Sorority Row* (Dir. Stewart Hendler) is a remake of *The House on Sorority Row* (Dir. Mark Rosman, 1982), which is not as well known or as well-loved as *Black Christmas* (1974), but it has its

ARIEL POWERS-SCHAUB

fans. Slasher fans who dig into everything from the '80s will have seen the original. Both "sorority row" films have a similar setup: sorority sisters are preparing to throw a big house party. A prank goes wrong, resulting in death, and the sorority sisters are picked off one by one in a whodunit. Other than the setup, the two films are quite different. The original has a strangeness to it you could only find in the '80s, and the acting is of variable quality. The 2009 remake feels much like the 2006 *Black Christmas*, in that it has a shiny veneer over a downright nasty plot.

*Sorority Row* begins during the school year, with a group of sorority sisters playing a prank on one of their boyfriends. They learned Garret (Matt O'Leary) had been cheating on Megan (Matt O'Leary), and Megan's friends hatch a plan. They give Garret roofies (sedatives to put in her drink) to use on Megan, and the fact that he accepts this idea is horrible on its own. Megan is in on the prank, and she pretends that the roofies have killed her. Garret panics, and Megan's friends play along, insisting they must go dump her body or they will all go to jail. Before the prank is revealed to Garret, and all the women have a chance to laugh at him, he accidentally actually kills Megan, and now the group has a real dead body on their hands, and very real panic. They decide to dump Megan's body, as they had been pretending they would do and agree never to tell anyone. Come spring and the final graduation party, and someone in a hooded robe is stalking and killing the women involved. Eventually, it's revealed that the killings were a misguided attempt by one of their boyfriends to help, so his girlfriend would be free of the guilt. The three Final Girls kill him and walk away triumphantly with the sorority house burning down behind them. It ends with a stinger that suggests a sequel that never came to fruition. It offers some brutal kills, often mixed with nudity, as you can expect of a slasher at this time.

It's a standard, almost textbook, slasher plot, and horror fans can probably rattle off several slashers that have a similar progression. What makes *Sorority Row* a Millennial Nasty is how the film executes those pilot points. In a standard of the time, sexual assault, abuse, and harassment are never taken as seriously as they should be. At its most harmless, it is male horniness played for laughs, like a man looking up a woman's skirt while she's on a ladder. At its worst, it's a psychiatrist demanding sex from his patients in exchange for drugs, or a boyfriend who believes that his girlfriend's friends would give him roofies meant for her. The initial prank hinges on the fact that the women are sure he will take the chance to drug his girl-friend, and if they believe that, they should encourage her to break up with him. The reveal that it was all for a prank doesn't make their actions any better, because rape is still a joke to them. In a final, misogynistic act of punishment, the killer stabs Jessica (Leah Pipes) through the mouth near the end of the film and says, "That girl really needs to learn to keep her mouth shut." A man telling a woman to be quiet, while also killing her with a phallic symbol in the mouth, may be an unintentional combination of factors, but they can't be ignored under scrutiny.

While this film plays sexual assault as a joke, it shames women for being sexual. The character that receives the brunt of the shaming is Chugs (Margo Harshman). Chugs's friends are constantly calling her a slut, and she plays into it. And maybe she does love sex, but it seems like she might be playing into the jokes as a defense mechanism. Her psychiatrist demands sex in exchange for pills, and she looks in the mirror and says "cheers, slut" before chugging some wine and going to make the exchange. It doesn't seem like she wants to be as sexual as everyone else assumes she does. One of Chugs's first lines in the movie, when they are watching the prank take place, is, "Roofie sex isn't that bad, you get laid, and you get a good night's sleep." She could just be joking to shock her friends, or she could be hiding from the pain of her own experiences. Her death is the most memorable, and it's noticeably sexualized. While lying down, her wine bottle is shoved down her throat, and she chokes on the liquid while the bottle cuts her from the inside. Almost as if to say, "you wouldn't be in this position if it were for drinking and sex." At the same time Chugs is being teased for how much sex she supposedly has, Ellie's (Rumer Willis) friends are always picking on her for "not getting laid." It's a frustrating double-edged sword that was very apparent in the media. Women were supposed to be sexy, and enjoy sex privately, but not supposed to be overtly sexual, or enjoy sex *too* much. It's an impossible standard. And our culture is not perfect, but we are at least better at discussing this double standard today. In a slasher, we can expect some sex and nudity - after all, sex leads to death in slashers. But *Sorority Row* is centered on female bodies, and everyone looking sexy all the time. The friends are mean to each other, like in *Black Christmas*, so we are meant to cheer for their deaths. The meanest, shallowest ones die, and the nicest ones live.

## Beware the Sorority House

Both *Black Christmas* and *Sorority Row* have common aesthetics, with the beautiful and polished look reminiscent of '90s slashers. What makes them Millennial Nasties is the meanness, edginess, and the post-'90s hatred of women that had become commonplace. Some filmmakers must have thought that horror audiences were all young men who wanted to see women die. Thankfully, other voices in the horror fandom have risen since then, and it's clearer than ever before that horror is for everyone, and many kinds of films can satisfy viewers. We don't need to cater only to the bros.

Interestingly, class commentary is light in these two films.

While the two sorority houses feature women who clearly come from more or less money - some girls have jobs, some have family money - they are all privileged enough to be in college. There is no fear of a recession, no worry about what they will do after they graduate. These women come to fear making it to graduation without being killed. In a whodunit slasher, it's not a fear of The Other like might be present in a folk horror, and often the killer ends up being someone close to the victims or someone local. Police are not heroes in either film - they are pretty much absent, and the sorority girls are on their own, plus a house mother. The only ones who come to their rescue are each other, and there is an uplifting message of sisterhood in there somewhere.

Slashers are usually punishment stories, but these two films take the punishment of women to a new level. In *Black Christmas*, the women are simply existing, and being killed for that. Newer slashers are often more subversive and rework old tropes into something new, and it's basically impossible not to be meta at this point. But even if we make it out of the sorority house, we may still find…

# HORROR CLOSE TO HOME

### Dawn of the Dead (2004), Halloween (2007), Halloween II (2009) and The Last House on the Left (2009)

Some of the remakes of this time period focused on stories that upset the comfortable domestic space. Not in the way a home invasion movie does–the films in this chapter have a different feeling than *The Strangers* (2008) and *The Collector* (2009) because while the horror is close to home, it's not all inside the home. Each of these stories takes the comfort of being at home and turns it on its head. In some cases, home is taken away, and in many cases, family is also lost. Indeed, the reimagining of these stories encapsulates the fear so many were feeling at this time, with their loved ones at war and their sense of safety upended after 9/11.These are horrors that take place in your town and are hard to escape by simply leaving. These horrors will follow the survivors and bring them discomfort for a long time.

### *Dawn of the Dead* (2004)

"America always sorts its shit out."

Similar to its 1978 original counterpart from George Romero, the characters in Zack Snyder's remake take shelter in a shopping mall to escape a zombie plague sweeping America. Unlike some self-aware zombie movies that become popular years later, the people in *Dawn of the Dead* (2004) do not use the word zombie, they don't know what zombies are, and they are learning how to survive through trial and error. There are initially two factions that have to work together - the mall security guards, who seem like horrible people at first, trying to turn away other survivors, and the group of strangers who found each other while looking for help and want to work together. In the mall, they are trying to create a home after their homes have been taken over by zombies. They spread out and find new clothes, real beds to sleep on, and they have family-style meals. Throughout the course of the film, most of them eventually work together and fight for survival. But what makes 2004's *Dawn of the Dead* unique and notable is how nasty it is, and the values it champions.

The themes in the film reflect American fears and feelings of the early 2000s after the 9/11 terrorist attacks. This film is very pro-America, pro-military, and pro-Christianity. Sometimes, that's presented in bigoted ways, such as the security guard CJ (Michael Kelly) saying, about the mall, "If we start letting people in here, then we're gonna let the wrong ones in." While I don't think the film itself is racist, that line efficiently represents the othering and racism displayed by some Americans of the time. (Not that bigotry is fixed now, but xenophobia was particularly prominent right after 9/11.) In another scene, there is an evangelical Christian preacher on TV (played by Ken Foree, in a nod to the original), saying that Hell has come to America because of sex before marriage, abortion, and same-sex relationships. This is, sadly, an all-too-real depiction of how some Evangelical Christians react to tragedy, blaming it on populations they want to attack, anyway. Similar to CJ's comment on border control, I don't think the film itself thinks premarital sex and queerness are to blame for the zombie apocalypse, but the dialogue serves as another reflection of how some Americans were reacting to tragedy.

Some of the characters seem to be, at best, desensitized to violence, and at worst, leaning into it as a coping mechanism. CJ and another security guard, Bart (Michael Barry), are watching violence on the news and rooting for it, laughing at the zombies (who were human moments ago) as they twitch and die. In the *Dawn of the Dead* remake, cops are heroes, and guns are necessary and good. Ving Rhames plays Kenneth, a police officer, who saves many lives and holds the group together - sometimes with force, sometimes with tough love, but Kenneth's goodness is never questioned. The group stockpiles all the guns and ammunition they can, and they befriend the owner of the gun store across the street. They reinforce buses with armor, and they stockpile extra gas to make explosives. The meaning of this is clear: fight for your lives with whatever weapons you have. As the group makes their final escape, they save themselves with giant explosions.

Another theme explored in this film is how an individual's attitude toward death can change, depending on their experiences. When they are first realizing that zombie bites create more zombies, one character, Frank (Matt Frewer), begs for the last moments of his life. He doesn't want to be shot until he's actually a zombie. As his face is turning gray, he croaks out, "You want every final second." Later in the film, as the group is trying to decide on a plan, Kenneth says, "There's some things worse than death, and one of them is sitting here, waiting to die." After witnessing so much carnage, he would rather go down fighting than waiting for death to come to him. That is the opposite of Frank's attitude. However, Frank and Kenneth had different experiences that lead them to their philosophies on death. In the end, the movie posits that sacrificing yourself for others is a good thing, especially for redemption and atonement. CJ, who has been antagonistic for most of the movie, sacrifices himself for the group as they are making their last-ditch effort to get off land and onto a boat.

The most prominent theme in the film is about trying to regain a sense of control. One of the earliest scenes in the film is the main protagonist, Ana (Sarah Polley), looking around her neighborhood as the carnage begins. Her beautiful, green, once quiet suburban neighborhood is now awash in chaos - fires, screaming, bleeding, zombies everywhere. She focuses on her skills as a nurse and helping others through the tragedy to regain a sense of control. Similarly, CJ focuses on his work. He feels comfortable in his role as a security guard, and he orders everyone to follow the regular rules of the mall, and he threatens anyone who might dare to steal. It seems like stolen inventory should be the least of his worries, but it's something he feels he can control. Eventually, as the direness of the situation becomes clearer, he lightens up a little and lets the group use items in the mall without paying for them. Both Ana and CJ fell back on the skills they knew well and things they could control in a chaotic situation.

One of the nastiest aspects of this film comes from trying to stay in control. Luda (Inna Korobkina) and Andre (Mekhi Phifer) are a married couple, and Luda is pregnant with their first child, and near the point of giving birth. Luda is bitten before anyone realizes the bites spread the zombie disease, so Luda and Andre don't make a point to tell anyone about her bite. Predictably, Luda starts to appear sick, her skin changing color and an infected wound. Andre is so focused on becoming a father, and he tells Kenneth his purpose is to bring his child into the world. All Andre has left of his previous life is the idea of being a dad, and he holds onto it at all costs. When Andre learns that the bites spread the disease, he doesn't tell Luda. Instead, he ties her to a bed in the area of the mall they have claimed and keeps others from visiting her. By the time she has the baby, Luda is fully transformed into a snarling, biting zombie. The childbirth scene is violent and bloody, a horrible tableau that can only get worse. The lighting is green, high-lighting the sickly feeling in the room. Luda is shot in the head, and Andre is shot and killed by another character. The only one left alive when others come running toward the gunshots is the zombie baby, wrapped in a pink blanket, and clearly undead. It's a horrifying reveal that Luda had a zombie baby inside her all along. There were no good options after Luda was bitten. The baby is shot and killed, thankfully off-screen, as a pro-Christian movie can't show the killing of a baby, even a zombie baby.

Nastiness in this film definitely comes in the form of gore and violence. Guns and other weapons are used liberally, and zombie heads explode for the viewers' enjoyment. One of the most memorable scenes is the first zombie we see - a little girl named Vivian (Hannah Lochner) - chomps the neck off of Ana's husband. The bite is stringy and bloody, and the camera doesn't shy away. The zombies look mean and gnarly, with discolored skin and eyes, and they run almost inhumanly fast. There is an excellent scene, with several zombies burning to death in slow motion. But a lot of nastiness also comes from the bleakness of the film. Before we see Ana's husband die, we learn they have a sweet and loving relationship, which makes his death hurt that much more. The survivors in the mall and the shop owner across the street make up a game where they shoot zombies that look like certain celebrities, just for fun. It's dark that the survivors went so quickly to seeing zombies as non-humans, but it might have been a necessary coping mechanism to survive in their new reality. Still, hunting humanoids for sport shows a numbness to the situation. The ending of the film is as bleak as it gets. The few survivors left make it to a boat and onto an island they think will be deserted, but it's already overrun with zombies. There is no escape, and all that fighting for their lives was futile. There is a gray-blue lighting over the ending of the movie, similar to the skin of the zombies, which gives the feeling of finality and despair, like running out of light.

While the filmmaking is more indicative of an action movie than a horror film, there are similarities to the other Millennial Nasty horrors of the time. The two main settings in the film, the hospital in the beginning and the mall for the majority of the film, are excessively green. The color casts a feeling of sickness over the whole film and contributes to the weight of the outbreak pressing down on the characters.

There are zombie scenes which bring the horror. For example, when Ana has to escape out a window from her husband, and when the survivors unknowingly bring an infected woman into the mall who transforms in front of their eyes. The audience feels suspense, because we know what transmits the zombie disease, and the characters do not. However, the best filmmaking is reserved for action scenes, like the dramatic shootouts and explosions.

This remake leveraged the fears and worries of Americans at the time - that our systems were failing us, and we could only arm and protect ourselves - and used it to make an enjoyable action-horror remake.

### *Halloween* (2007)

"He has come back for his baby sister."

Rob Zombie's 2007 remake of the 1978 classic John Carpenter's *Halloween* is one of the most divisive remakes among fans of the original. Somehow, the two films are both very different and very similar films. The first act of the remake spends more time with young Michael (Daeg Faerch) and his family, and after the initial murder of his family, focuses on Dr. Loomis's (Malcolm McDowell) treatment of Michael. Mrs. Myers (Sheri Moon Zombie) kills herself when she realizes Michael is not making any progress. The focus on Michael's family is a big departure from the original plot. In the 1978 film, Michael Myers is also known as The Shape (played by Tony Moran), because he is such a mysterious figure, and you can project all your fears onto him. The rest of the movie is almost a beat-for-beat remake of the events of the original. Laurie (Scout Taylor-Compton), Annie (Danielle Harris) and Lynda (Kristina Klebe) are stalked and attacked by Michael while babysitting on Halloween night. Annie is played by Danielle Harris, who fans will remember from *Halloween 4: The return of Michael Myers* (Dir. Dwight H. Little, 1988). There are scenes taken from the original and recreated, such as Michael wearing a sheet and glasses to trick Lynda before he kills her, and the three friends walking home from school on a sidewalk covered with autumn leaves. The ending of the remake differs from the original: in the remake Laurie pulls the trigger on the bullet that ends Michael (for now) and has an ending like Sally Hardesty (played by Marilyn Burns), screaming, crying, and covered in blood. Annie survives, and Laurie doesn't have to be the only final girl, unlike in the 1978 film. Another important difference between this film and its original is the familial relationship. In the original timeline, it's not revealed until *Halloween II* (1981) that Michael and Laurie are related. In Rob Zombie's remakes, that's a clear plot point from the beginning, though it's a secret kept from Laurie.

The themes explored in this film are fairly straightforward: family, secrets, trauma, and severe mental illness. Michael comes from a chaotic and unhappy home, and while he likely has some untreated illness, his home life is not helping, and everything converges to make him the masked killer he becomes. Laurie is removed from that same home as a baby, and seems to be doing well as a teenager, but she cannot escape her past. Her past is a secret from her, and she has no idea why Michael is attacking her and her friends. Her past followed her to her new home and family.

The filmmaking offers a mix of familiar Rob Zombie preferences and pieces of the original film. The original iconic music is used, and while modified, it's recognizable. Sheri Moon Zombie plays Michael's mother, and other Zombie favorites, like Sid Haig and Danny Trejo, make appearances, like they do in other Zombie films. Michael commits his first murders in a clown costume in both films, but it's updated for a 1990s boy, and the mask is much creepier than the cute costume in 1978. When we see adult Michael in his room in the sanitarium, where he has been for fifteen years, the walls are covered in masks he made himself. It brings to mind the set dressing in *House of 1000 Corpses* (2003). In a wise, creepy filmmaking choice, we are never shown any other kids or families in the sanitarium. It offers a feeling of isolation, which makes the situation with Michael even tenser. The gross, unsettling feeling from the sets and the dialogue, mixed with the lore of the original Michael, all comes together to make a remake that feels both familiar and new.

Michael and Laurie are both excellent characters with great performances, including both young Michael and adult Michael (Tyler Mane). Young Michael is portrayed as sensitive, loving, and naïve. He loves his mom and his baby sister, and he tries to avoid the cruelty of his stepdad and older sister. He wants to be a normal kid, but he doesn't have the environment or encouragement to do so. Adult Michael is a huge, hulking figure, silent and scary, and Mane's performance delivers those attributes perfectly. Meanwhile, Laurie's character has an opposite arc. Her life is going well until Michael enters her teenage life. Laurie goes from a bright, happy, studious teen, giggling about boys and hanging out with her parents, to a scared, confused, sprinting final girl in a matter of moments. An aspect of the film that doesn't work as well as the rest of it is Michael's motivation. When he comes back as an adult, it's not clear how he decides who to stalk, who to kill quickly, and who to kill slowly and painfully. If Michael's motivation is just to get to his baby sister, it would make sense to quickly kill everyone in his way. If his motivation is to hurt people, it would make sense to torture everyone. Since Michael is a person with a backstory, and not just The Shape, his unclear motivation stands out.

I remember hearing criticism at the time of this film's release from horror fans who didn't like this film. Some of it was the standard criticism lobbed at torture porn and at remakes, of which this film is both, so fans were going to scrutinize it no matter what. But I remember hearing additional criticism because Zombie was more focused on the killer rather than victims, which was seen as a disrespectful way to frame the story. I don't agree with that criticism. It's true that Michael Myers is much more fleshed-out in the 2007 remake and its sequel in 2009. But fleshing out Michael doesn't mean anything is taken away from Laurie or the other victims. Zombie gave Michael some backstory as a person, instead of making him The Shape and the pure embodiment of evil. For some, a regular person going on a killing spree is scarier than the abstract idea of evil incarnate. At the same time, Laurie is an amazing character in this film. She is still the "good girl" in her friend group, opting to watch the neighborhood kids so her friends can drink and have sex on Halloween. But she also fights ferociously and saves herself. She is scared, and she screams and cries and runs, and doesn't do everything perfectly, but she is a Final Girl you can root for.

But it's not all thoughtful and hopeful. On the contrary, this film earns its Millennial Nasty title through its dialogue, sex, and violence. The dialogue is gross, mean, and over-the-top, especially in young Michael's home. It plainly shows the chaotic environment he's living in. As in many Rob Zombie films, the dialogue doesn't necessarily represent how real people speak most of the time, but the characters are written purposefully, and the performances are strong. The dialogue normalizes a bit when we get to the "present day" part of the story. There is a lot of overt sexuality in this film. Some of it fits into a slasher framework just fine - such as seeing naked breasts when a couple is having sex. But some of it is extra-nasty, such as Judith

Myers's stepfather commenting on her nice ass. The kill scenes of the teenage girls are sexualized. Annie's chase scene and the attack she survives takes place while she is topless, and there are many shots of her breasts covered in blood. Lynda is killed completely naked. And, as in the original, Judith Myers is killed after having sex with her boyfriend. Though the "sex equals death" formula is standard in slashers, often the scenes were quick, and you didn't see much nudity and gore. Millennial Nasties wanted to shock in any way they could, including sexualizing death. The deaths for women are much worse in this film than they are for the men. For example, Laurie's father is killed quickly, but her mother's death is drawn out for the camera. In the director's cut, there is a violent rape scene before Michael breaks out of the hospital, perpetrated not by Michael but by hospital staff on another patient. Michael's life is heartbreaking, which doesn't excuse his horrible actions, but it does inform them. His mother hangs on for as long as she can, after both her husband and her eldest daughter are dead, trying to encourage her son. But she ultimately dies by suicide because it becomes too much.

The plot points, dialogue, and visuals in this film make the perfect mix for a nasty remake.

Though Laurie survives, she is clearly and understandably broken at the end of the film. There is so much screaming and shaky-cam in the last act of this film, it puts the audience on edge. *Halloween* 1978 doesn't leave you feeling sick and hopeless, but the 2007 remake sure can.

### *Halloween II* (2009)

"I'm Michael Myers's sister! I'm so fucked!"

Similar to Rick Rosenthal's 1981 film, Rob Zombie's remake of *Halloween 2* starts on the same night the first film ended. But that's where the similarities end. The 2009 sequel feels much more like Rob Zombie has the freedom to use his own ideas and explore something new. The story follows Laurie and Annie one year after the events of the first film (or two years after, on the director's cut). Laurie is not doing well, having constant nightmares and breaking down in therapy. She's been living with Annie and Annie's dad, Sheriff Brackett (Brad Dourif), since her own parents were killed. Michael's body was lost when the vehicle transporting it crashed, and it was never recovered. Laurie worries that he's still out there and coming for her. Meanwhile, Dr. Loomis survived, and is on an extremely successful book tour. He's turned mean and cynical, and he is thoughtlessly making money off the back of a tragedy. Laurie picks up a copy of the book and reads the truth no has bothered to tell her: that she and Michael are siblings. She breaks down, yells at Annie, and runs out to a Halloween party to get drunk with her other group of friends. The film ends in a confrontation between her and Michael, and depending on which version of the film you watch, Laurie either lives or dies. In the theatrical version, she ends up isolated in psychiatric care, just like her brother was. In the director's cut, she's shot and killed by police.

The main theme explored in this film is how different people cope and survive after trauma. Laurie is the biggest example, as our main protagonist. After surviving her horrific Halloween night, she doesn't look, act, or seem like the girl we met in the previous film. Her blond hair is long and scraggly, like her long-lost brother's. She's made a new group of friends, where she can be a different version of herself, because they didn't live through the worst night of her life with her. They are more than willing to drink and party with her, whereas Annie is more of a homebody now. Especially in the director's cut, you can tell how much Laurie's life has spiraled. She is drinking and avoiding her feelings as much as possible. Annie, on the other hand, seems to be managing alright. Not like she forgot everything that happened to her, but that she is coping well. She seems more mature than she was in the first film, and more content to have a night in with her dad. She lectures him about eating healthily, and tries to keep Laurie safe, perhaps more concerned than ever about losing her loved ones. Loomis has decided to use the tragedy for his own benefit and turn it into a money-making opportunity. While it's not inherently immoral to make money telling the story of your trauma, he's disregarding the feelings of others, and being cocky and crass to those around him. At one point, he says to a colleague offering him criticism, "When I want your opinion, I'll beat it out of you." He is ignoring his own trauma associated with treating Michael and then confronting him. He's acting like a completely different person, because he wishes he was. At his book signing, Lynda's dad comes to his table and confronts him, threatening him with a gun, which is a short but accurate representation of another way to respond to trauma: with anger.

Another theme explored briefly but efficiently is about fan obsession. This brings to mind fans of killers in films, such as Michael Myers, or actual true-crime obsessed people who make lists of their "favorite" serial killers. When Loomis is at his book signing, an exuberant fan comes up and says, "Michael is so much deeper than those other guys, like Dahmer and that bitch Bundy." He sounds like he admires Michael and looks up to him. Loomis quickly shoos him away, and says to the crowd of people waiting, "There's always one." It's a tight scene to quickly poke fun at the fans who got too obsessed with Michael Myers in real life, and Zombie holding up a mirror form them.

And of course, with Rob Zombie, there is no shortage of nastiness throughout. *Halloween II* has much more of the Rob Zombie-style atmosphere than the first one did. Michael's dead mom appears to him in visions, looking like an angel with a white horse. There are several dream-like sequences with young Michael and adult Michael together, talking to his mother through Young Michael. Some of the dreamlike sequences have a music-video-feeling in their editing, much like *House of 1000*

*Corpses* (2003). Nearly all the sets are gritty and dark. There is almost no sunshine, no happiness or fun. Even Laurie's new friends seem to be on the edge of meanness most of the time. After most of the kills, there are a few moments of silence, as if we are in Michael's head, and nothing is there. Annie's chase scene and ultimately her death have a much different feeling than her attack in the first film. *In Halloween II*, it's a slow-motion chase, and the kill is mostly heard rather than shown. It's not the titillating, topless, running-around-the-house-screaming scene we saw before. It's a young woman running for her life when she has no chance of survival. Laurie has to find Annie, not quite dead, and hold her best friend while she dies. It's brutal. In addition to creative kill scenes - like smashing someone's head into glass over and over again until she is unrecognizable - there are other kinds of gross out moments. Michael eats a freshly dead dog, raw, scooping hand-fuls into his mouth. The coroner's staff are making jokes about having sex with Lynda's corpse. We see Laurie in surgery, and a closeup of a fingernail being removed. Around every turn, Zombie finds a way to make us gag or cringe, or both.

*Halloween II* ended Zombie's *Halloween* remakes (for now, anyway, who knows what the future holds). It makes sense to end the story here - in the director's cut, Laurie and Michael are both dead; their story is sadly over.

### *The Last House on the Left* (2009)

"We have to be prepared to do anything."

Directed by Dennis Iliadis and co-produced by Jonathan Craven (the son of the director of the original), the remake opens with scenes of a happy family. Mari (Sara Paxton) and her parents are on vacation in their remote lake house, when Mari and her friend Paige (Martha MacIsaac) decide to accompany a stranger, Justin (Spencer Treat Clark) to his motel room for some marijuana. He is a little awkward and shy, and Mari is hesitant to smoke, but eventually the three of them start to open up and have fun. That's when the adults come back - Justin's father, Krug (Garret Dillahunt), Justin's uncle, Francis (Aaron Paul), and Krug's girlfriend, Sadie (Riki Lindhome). They are on the run, having murdered police officers, and they kidnap the girls because they are afraid of being turned in to the police. While trying to escape, they end up in the woods, where the criminals kill Paige and rape Mari. They think Mari is dead, but she makes it back to her parents. Meanwhile, the killers seek refuge from the storm at the closest house, which they don't realize belongs to Mari's parents. When Mari makes it back, and her parents realize what has happened, they know they need to survive the night and get their daughter to safety, by any means necessary.

It's a similar plot to the 1972 original, Wes Craven's directorial debut, but the ambiance is different, and many horror fans prefer the remake. In the original, Mari dies, which leaves her parents with different options and priorities. The original has more of a comedic tone at times, pairing over-the-top slapstick comedy with the violence, and jaunty music over the scenes of rape and violence. The 2009 remake takes a more straightforward approach and feels like a horror film throughout.

The filmmaking is efficient and establishes the setting and characters before the terror starts. Mari's family is sweet and loving. Her parents are a little overprotective because they also had a son who passed away. They are awash in soft lighting and surrounded by light colors. Mari, the Final Girl, is in a light-colored tank top. Swimming is both her passion and her talent. She and her family are vacationing in a remote location - cell phones have little-to-no signal, storms can knock out power and phone lines for hours or even days. When the criminals arrive at Mari's home, the tension comes from the audience knowing how the two groups of characters connect, while the characters don't yet know. The audience knows the criminals hurt Mari and killed Paige, and we know the parents will find out sooner or later, and tension builds while time passes. As her parents begin to put the pieces together, the horror in their eyes grows, and you are seeing the tragedy through the eyes of a parent looking at their nearly dead child. After the parents realize what's happening, there are some sickly green scenes in the house at night, and the fight scenes between the adults are nothing short of epic. This movie is excellently made.

And within this excellent movie is a ton of nastiness. Let us first analyze the nastiest part, the rape scene in the woods. When the criminals are kidnapping Mari and Paige and driving away from the hotel, Mari causes them to crash in the woods just as she has gained their trust. The car, which belonged to Mari's parents, is totaled, and they are stranded. Furious, the criminals decide to torture and rape the girls, and ultimately, kill them. Anyone familiar with the original film knows this scene is coming, but waiting for it builds the viewers' discomfort. Paige is chased through the woods by Sadie, and the scene is shot in a way reminiscent of Sally's in *The Texas Chain Saw Massacre* (1974). When Paige is dragged back to the group, Sadie rips Paige's shirt. Frank kicks Mari in the stomach while she's on the ground. Krug asks his son, "You ready to be a man?" And instructs him to "pick one, or both." Justin freezes and refuses, and he's sitting on the sidelines while his family assaults the girls. Paige is stabbed in the stomach, between her bra and her navel piercing, and it's an unsexy penetrative act, like the imminent rape. She drops to the ground, left to bleed out of her stab wound. Mari holds Paige while she dies, and Krug taunts her with cruelty, encouraging her to promise Paige everything will be ok. Once Paige is dead, the criminals turn their focus to Mari.

Before Mari is undressed, Justin is forced to touch her breasts, as Krug tries again to get his son involved. When Justin refuses, he's again sidelined, and his dad calls him pathetic. Krug holds Mari face down on the ground, while Sadie removes

Mari's shorts and underwear, encouraging Krug by saying, "Look around, look at what she did." The rape scene goes on for several minutes in the unrated version, and it's difficult to watch, but it's a rape scene that is shot well. It's not shot to be titillating or sexy, which can be a problem with rape scenes in film. On the contrary, it's harrowing and disgusting. Most of the shots focus on Mari's face, or Justin's face, and the most nudity in the scene is the side of Krug's rear end. Mari cries and begs Justin for help, and the camera gives the viewer a break from watching the rape, with some shots of the surrounding woods. This is a respectable example of a well-done rape scene in cinema. While Mari and Paige are without a doubt the most violated in this scene, it's necessary to note that Justin is also violated here. He's a minor, and he's forced to touch someone sexually against his will and forced to watch and be party to rape. Of course, viewers can wish Justin acted differently in that scene, and tried to help Mari, but he likely knew that would make things worse for him. Freezing up can be a natural reaction to abuse, and he's trying to survive in an abusive family.

Sadie is an interesting character worthy of analysis in this scene. From the beginning of the film, it's clear that she's desperate for Krug's approval, and will do anything to get it, including murder. For example, Sadie and Francis help Krug escape police custody early in the film, and the end up killing two police officers. Sadie's biggest concern is Krug's approval, and after killing the cops, she pleads to him, "Tell me I did good." So, it's not completely surprising that she would encourage Krug to harm a teenage girl if she thought she could get his approval, even if it means encouraging rape. And she doesn't just encourage Krug, she psychically participates in the rape. Some viewers think Sadie is the most morally reprehensible of the group, because she is a woman. Often, sexual abuse at the hands of women can be held to a different standard, and the message is "women should know better because they should be afraid of abuse." A horror fan might be more accustomed to seeing men commit fictional on-screen rape, and seeing a woman take part is a bridge too far for some, whether or not that's a fair standard.

After the rape, Krug disgustingly tells Justin, "You missed out." Mari stands up very slowly and shakily, in both physical and mental anguish. She's dressing herself, covered in dirt from the forest floor, and crying. She says, under her breath, "I swim." Sadie asks her to repeat herself, and Mari says, a little louder, "I love to swim." The criminals disregard this, but it's an important line. Practically, it reminds the audience that Mari has another route to get away, by swimming in the lake. But perhaps even more importantly, Mari is immediately affirming to herself who she is, that she is still herself, even after the rape. Her body can do something amazing and impressive, a skill she has purposefully developed over the years. Her body is still hers, and no one can take that away from her. She still has things in the world she loves. It's an extremely powerful message to send after an on-screen rape, that the survivor can get back up and find herself again. Mari hits Krug on the head with a rock and runs to the lake. As she's swimming away, Krug shoots her, and they assume she's dead. Krug and Francis walk away, but Sadie stays behind and looks on for a little longer, with a regretful look on her face. Maybe she is having doubts about her actions, but she turns and follows the men.

Outside of the rape scene, there is other violence and nudity that puts this film in Millennial Nasty territory and fills out the rest of the film. It opens with a violent act, when Francis and Sadie break Krug out of the cop car. The deaths of the cops are violent and nasty, one of them forced to look at pictures of kids while he bleeds on them and dies. The entire motel scene is disturbing, and reminiscent of the motel scene in *The Devil's Rejects* (2005) when the Firefly Family is torturing the musicians they met. When Paige and Mari are in the motel room, Paige is threatened with a knife. The door is blocked, and the viewer knows the girls could die right then and there. The killings of the criminals near the end of the film are cathartic, violent deaths, earned by their actions earlier in the story. Sadie is shot through the eye, and dies with her breasts out, just so the movie could get in a little more nudity. Francis dies in a fight with Mari's parents, after his hand is chewed up by the garbage disposal. And because he taunted her parents about what he did to Mari, Krug is kept alive so Mari's dad can first paralyze him and then kill him with a faulty microwave.

The themes explored in this film are all about family and survival. Two profoundly different families are portrayed - Mari's family, and Justin's family. Justin is abused, threatened, and constantly afraid. Mari is loved. Her parents care about her wellbeing, and they prove that they will do anything for her. This is a rape-revenge movie where the revenge is not sought by the survivor of rape, but by her parents. After the rape scene, Mari is barely in the film, and it becomes a story about her parents. It's heartbreaking while her father, a doctor, lovingly cleans her bullet wound, and as he's treating her, realizes she's been raped. In the end, Mari and her parents survive, and they escape on the boat with Justin. They show mercy and empathy by seeing Justin as a victim in this situation, too.

Mari's will to live and how hard she fights for survival are uplifting themes in an otherwise dark film. She swims with a bullet in her back, and makes it to her parents' porch, where they find her. She purposely crashes the car in a part of the woods she is familiar with, so she has a chance at escaping. She fights and pushes through after the worst hours of her life. It's both horrible and powerfully inspiring.

## HOME IS WHAT YOU FIGHT FOR

The films in this chapter consider different reactions to survival and trauma, and the fear of having the comfort of home disrupted and destroyed. Or perhaps home never was comfortable, and characters like Justin and young Michael show their struggles in those environments. Even if you can establish a comfortable home and loving family, you need to watch where you find yourself, because ...

# THE LOCALS RUN THIS TOWN

The Texas Chainsaw Massacre (2003), House of Wax (2005), and The Hills Have Eyes (2006)

Horror has always loved stories about stumbling into where you don't belong, finding yourself in an unwelcoming place. Fear of The Other is relatable, because there is always someone different from oneself. The remakes of this era flourished on feeding this fear, and these three films offer excellent examples of towns where you don't want to meet the locals. Whether it's groups of naïve teenagers, or a family trying to enjoy a vacation, characters feel entitled to all the spaces they come across, and they learn the hard way those spaces aren't meant for them.

## *The Texas Chainsaw Massacre* (2003)

"What you do is your own business."

The 2003 remake, directed by Marcus Nispel, has a similar setup to Tobe Hooper's 1974 original. A vanful of young people are on the road in Texas, and a series of missteps lead them to

Leatherface and his family. Beyond that setup, this version of the film adds more backstory to the iconic villain and family, makes different choices with some of the characters, and has more graphic violence. It opens with narration, as does the original, but this time it's over grainy police file footage, recovered after the cops went missing investing Leatherface and his family. The opening footage adds a cinematic scariness to the beginning of the film that nods to the original.

Two couples - Erin (Jessica Biel) and Kemper (Eric Balfour), and Andy (Mike Vogel) and Pepper (Erica Leerhsen), plus their friend Morgan (Jonathan Tucker), are on their way to a Lynyrd Skynyrd concert. The group of friends stops to help a young woman on the side of the road (credited as "teenage girl," portrayed by Lauren German), who panics when she sees what direction they are driving and shoots herself in the head. The friends, especially Erin, want to find help instead of just dumping her body and moving on, and that's how they end up on Leatherface's farm. The friends are killed off one by one, save for our Final Girl Erin in the white tank top, who also saves a kidnapped infant on her way out.

While the original film was a response to violence in the world, especially the Vietnam War, this film explores other kinds of themes. There is a fear of The Other who is different from "us," which is often explored in folk horror. The pretty, young adults with enough money to go to a Lynyrd Skynyrd concert are confronted by the dirty underbelly of rural and poor America. Most likely it's unintentional, but this film perpetuates stereotypes against people from the country, especially through the eyes of people from the city. There is also the exploration of what it means to do "the right thing" and when you should care for others versus yourself. Erin is the most vocal about wanting to help the woman on the side of the road, and about taking her body to the police instead of abandoning her and driving away. She convinces her friends the right thing to do is to see it through and do the best they can for this person they don't know. Some of her friends are very vocal against taking responsibility for the body every step of the way. Perhaps the film is saying Erin gets to survive because she did "the right thing," and her friends had to die because they were more hesitant. Or perhaps the lesson is "don't help strangers and keep yourself safe."

The film feels like a cross between the 1970s and the 2000s, but in a confused way rather than purposeful. The clothes are like what modern kids in the 2000s would have worn for '70s day at school, rather than the authentic clothes of the 1970s. It's a subtle but noticeable difference to those of us who grew up in the 2000s. This film owes more to the glossy slashers of the '90s than it does to the grittiness of '70s grindhouse films - it's beauty dirtied-up, as if a fashion model had to do a photo shoot looking filthy. First, they make it beautiful, then they throw some dust on top. Whereas the original film makes the audience feel like they can smell the hot, rotting meat and feel the dirt under their nails, the 2003 remake feels much safer. This might have been the right choice, in 2003, when horror audiences were just coming down from the slasher boom and *Saw* (2004) hadn't hit the big screen yet.

One of the most memorable shots is of Erin, walking toward the farmhouse, and the camera is behind. It's meant to be reminiscent of the shot of Pam (Teri McMinn) in the original, but it misses the point of the original shot. I do not know if this is an intentional choice to cater to 2000s audiences, or if the filmmakers had a different idea about what that shot of Pam means. In the original film, Pam is filmed from behind, in her red shorts and a halter top that exposed her back. She is to the right of the frame, and the house and the land are central. It's shot from below, distorting the perspective, and making Pam and the house the same size. This shot conveys how alone and exposed Pam is. It's important that we see her bare back, because when she is later hung on a meat hook, it's much more brutal after we have seen her vulnerable body. Viewers often think they see more gore in Pam's death, but we don't actually see the hook go into her back, we just imagine it. Part of the movie magic is planting her exposed back in our heads with this shot. The shot of pam walking to the house is not sexy, it's unsettling. Pam is sexy, of course, and that can't be hidden away, but it's not the purpose of the shot. The parallel shot in the remake shoots Erin from behind, and focus is straight on her rear end. The fore-shadowing and vulnerability are lost. The new version of the shot is just about showing us how sexy Jessica Biel is. It's almost unfair to compare any film to the original *Texas Chain Saw Massacre*, because it's such an iconic and adored film. And the comparison of these two shots, one meant to pay homage to the other, highlights the difference in filmmaking between the two films.

There are some filmmaking decisions that accentuate this film's place between the '90s and what was to come later in the 2000s - especially in the lighting. There is beautiful, almost serene, lighting in the woods at night, when Erin is running away from the killers. The gorgeous scenery brings to mind the glossy style of '90s slashers. This is in stark contrast to Sally's chase scene in the original, iconically portrayed by Marilyn Burns, where the woods were dark and eating her alive. The dazzling lighting in the remake feels out of place in the *Texas Chainsaw* world. However, there are filmmaking choices that highlight this film's place in the decade. Erin in her white tank top, especially. The design of Leatherface (played by Andrew Bryniarski) is appropriately nasty. He's huge, filthy, and his masks keep falling apart. The sets in the film offer plenty of nastiness. Leatherface's workshop seems to be a large basement or cellar, and everything is dirty and wet. This is the only set in the film that evokes a similar feeling to the original, like you might actually be able to smell the rot and decay through your TV. The workshop is also where there is some green and yellow lighting used, a style about to get much more popular later in the decade. During one of Erin's chase scenes, she hides inside a dead animal hung on a meat hook. In the gas station, where the group of friends stops for help, there is a disgusting meat counter - unrefrigerated pig heads and other animal parts sit in the hot room behind a dirty window and serve as a hangout for flies. Inside the family home, there is random meat, or maybe just skin, hanging to dry, and there are loose live chickens and pigs running through the house. Buckets of blood are randomly placed throughout, as if the inhabitants don't know where their domestic living space ends and their work begins. Maybe it's all one and the same.

The kills are violent and brutal and serve as perfect examples early in the decade of the nastiness to come. When the hitchhiker shoots herself through the head, the camera follows the bullet in a tracking shot through the gaping hole in her head and out the back window, set to the screams of the passengers in the van. This is when the film sets the audience's expectations. Erin and her friends have to drive around with the dead body, stinking and flopping in the seat, for quite a while before they can get someone to take it. The Sheriff (R. Lee Ermey), who is also a member of Leatherface's family, adds even more disgust to the idea of a dead body in the van. As he helps the guys wrap up the corpse, he talks about fondling corpses of good-looking women while on the job. Another kill that's painful to watch is Andy's. It takes a long time, because he is hung on the meat hook in Leatherface's workshop while he's still alive. He tries to pull himself free, only to re-hang himself on the hook and cause more pain. Erin eventually finds him and tries to save him, only to have the same thing happen, and he meets the pressure of the hook for the third time. Finally, Erin mercy-kills him by stabbing in the stomach, which covers her in blood, and Andy dies hanging on a meat hook with his arms outstretched.

This was a divisive remake, especially for fans of the original. It has quite a prominent torture porn feel; the characters are less likable than in the original, and it gives Leatherface more backstory. It's gotten a reappraisal in recent years, and more horror fans are warming up to it. Taken on its own, it's a strong folk-slasher that tries new things with classic framing.

### *House of Wax* (2005)

> "You can get used to anything if you're
> around it long enough."

It's hard to compare 2005's *House of Wax* to an original, because it's influenced by several stories that came before. There's the 1933 film *Mystery of the Wax Museum* (Dir. Michael Curtiz), which was remade in 1953 and titled *House of Wax* (Dir. Andre DeToth). The 2005 film also owes a lot to 1979's *Tourist Trap* (Dir. David Schmoeller). The 2005 film borrows story elements of these films that came before and adds modern plot points to make it interesting for 2005 audiences. It starts with a group of friends on a road trip, as so many folk horror slashers do. There are six friends, which is a relatively large group for a slasher road trip, and it's not just three couples. Carly (Elisha Cuthbert) and Wade (Jared Padalecki) are dating, Nick

(Chad Michael Murray) and Carly are twins. Paige (Paris Hilton) and Blake (Robert Ri'chard) are dating, and Dalton (Jon Abrahams) is there, too. They are on their way to a big football game in the rural American south. They have some car trouble (of course) and stop in a local neighborhood for help. The neighborhood is hidden and hard to find, as most of the roads are inaccessible, and it's not recorded on the map. Throughout the film, the group of friends finds reasons to split up, and each time they try to get back together, more of them have been killed. The secret of the town is that it's made entirely of wax, and only inhabited by the sons of Trudy, who ran the town's wax museum. There are wax figures used as props throughout the town to give it a lived-in look and trick the outsiders into thinking it's just a sleepy small neighborhood. The dirty secret is that the wax artists take human bodies and turn them into wax figures to display in the town.

The characters and friendships are more developed than you often see in slashers, and there is no shortage of backstory and plot. For example, one of the characters, Paige (Paris Hilton) thinks she might be pregnant, and is scared to tell her boyfriend. The main protagonist, Carly, is experiencing tension with her high school sweetheart because she plans to move to New York City for an internship and he doesn't want to go with her. Most of these plot points don't amount to much, since everyone but Carly and her twin brother die, but they give the story emotional stakes and instill empathy in these characters before they die. There could be themes explored about strong friendships, family relationships, sibling rivalry, and there is potentially a queer reading based on the friendship between two male characters, Nick and Dalton. The sibling rivalry idea is alluded to in the brothers who run the wax town, and in the film, they loop at the cinema, *What Ever Happened to Baby Jane?* (Dir. Robert Aldrich, 1962). However, there is no deep exploration of any of the characters' relationships, despite the nearly two-hour runtime. There are a lot of kills and melting wax to get to.

And get to them, we do. Though there isn't a real bit of terror until about fifty minutes in, there is some nastiness in the beginning to tide us over. The first shots of the film show a flashback to child abuse, which we learn later is the family of wax artists. There is also a scene in which Carly falls into a pit of rotting animal parts in the hot summer sun and sees a human hand (which turns out to be a prosthetic).

There are amazing scenes in which we get to see what happens to bodies covered in wax. Wade, Carly's boyfriend, is smothered by hot wax while he is still alive. His mouth is stitched shut, and he's literally showered with wax while he tries to scream. It's an excellent set piece, with several shower-heads pouring wax from different directions, in a room full of candles and bubbling pots. As a wax figure, he's propped up in the house, and discovered by Dalton, who sees Wade's eyes move and realizes he is still alive. Dalton has the terrible idea to pull the wax off, bringing chunks of Wade's cheek with it. It's a nasty, close, and slow scene, displaying an outcome worse than death. There is also body horror without wax in this film. When Carly is captured, the tip of her finger is chopped off with a bolt cutter as she tries to reach for help. Her mouth is super glued shut, and she has to pull her lips apart as they crack and bleed. Of course, as the Final Girl in the white tank top, she gets over these injuries quickly, and her bloody red lips just look like sexy lip-gloss by the end of the film.

For a film that bothered with so much backstory and plot for its characters, the best parts are the visuals. Everything is in service of the big set piece at the end of the film, when Trudy's House of Wax burns and melts to the ground. There are scenes both gross and scary, of people trying to climb stairs made of wax melting under their feet (it brings to mind the stairs in *A Nightmare on Elm Street* (Dir. Wes Craven, 1984)), and falling into scalding hot wax. There is flesh melting out of the once-alive humans who have been preserved as wax figures. Carly and Nick peeling their way out of the walls is unlike any other escape in a slasher film; it's tense, and it looks phenomenal.

It's impossible to discuss the nastiness of *House of Wax* without talking about the "See Paris Die" marketing campaign. Much of the film's marketing relied on posters that said See Paris Die with the release date of the film. There are plenty of photographs of Paris Hilton posing next to these posters. While we still don't always treat female celebrities with the respect and humanity they deserve, the 2000s were even worse. Attractive young, female celebrities, especially if you were famous for being famous, were under a mean amount of scru-tiny. (Even being famous for your talent didn't save you - look at what the public did to Britney Spears in 2007.) The amount of public vitriol directed at Paris Hilton was immense, and she likely didn't deserve most of it. When she was nineteen, she made a sex tape that was released on the internet without her consent in 2004. (In recent years, she has spoken about how she wasn't sober at the time and felt coerced by an older man to make the tape. She speaks about her shock and humiliation when the tape was out for everyone to see.) The public ate up this spectacle, and it fueled their hate for a young Hilton. Most likely to try to save her own image, and act like she could take a joke (though the joke shouldn't have been made), she played into the See Paris Die campaign with a smile on her face. The marketing campaign was brutally mean, and only recently have horror fans started to reckon with that and realize how hurtful it must have been. To twist the knife further, sex tape jokes are made in *House of Wax*, as the friend group has a camera and secretly tapes Paige probably performing oral sex on her boyfriend in the car, which they all laugh about. Later, during her death scene, the killer films it on that same camera, presumably to watch himself later, much like the purpose of the sex tape. The nastiness in the film matches the nastiness outside the film and exposes our orientation to young female celebrities of the time. To her great credit, Hilton does a fantastic job in her role. Her performance is strong, her character is interesting and - yes - her chase scene and her death are exciting and extraordinary. She made the absolute most she could out of a bad situation, and we got a great horror film.

Other filmmaking decisions place this Millennial Nasty firmly in 2005. Disturbed, Deftones, and Marilyn Manson are all on the soundtrack. There is the signature green and yellow coloring in the gas station and in the house. And there is plenty of bigotry in the dialogue. It has the slasher elements of kids acting like they own the world, just walking into places they don't belong and touching everything, and the small town that everyone left behind and forgot. But the combination of nastiness, storing characters, and the wax set pieces make this a standout among the genre of the time.

## *The Hills Have Eyes* (2006)

"You made us what we've become!"

Compared to Wes Craven's 1977 original, the remake of *The Hills Have Eyes* has a similar story. A family of mostly unlikable characters is on a road trip through the desert, and they crash their truck and trailer when they hit some spikes in the road, intentionally left out by cannibalistic hill people. They are miles from help in any direction, in the hot desert sun with little supplies, two dogs, and a baby. The hill people attack the family, presumably to turn them into food. The surviving family members have to fight back and hope to find an escape. The 2006 remake, directed by Alexandre Aja, adds reasoning to explain why the cannibalistic hill people are the way they are. The hill people in the 2006 version have been poisoned with radiation from nuclear testing done by the U.S. government, and to survive, they have become inbred cannibals. They chose not to leave their mining town. (If it sounds like a similar plot to *Wrong Turn* (2003), it sure is.)

It was produced by Wes Craven, who directed the original. He sought out Alexandre Aja to direct the remake. Aja had had recent success with the New French Extremity film *High Tension* (2003) (also known as *Switchblade Romance*) and he brought a similar level of grittiness to *The Hills Have Eyes*. Early in the film, it's established that there is no cell service in the desert, which is believable for the location and the time period. You can almost feel the dry, oppressive heat radiating through your TV. There is no shade, nowhere to hide from the sun, nowhere to hide from anyone in the sprawling desert.

The themes in this film are straightforward and typical of the time period - cops are heroes, guns are necessary, traditional masculinity is preferred. There is not much room left for more nuanced interpretation. The patriarch, Big Bob (Ted Levine), is a retired detective, and he runs his family like a supervisor, telling them what to do and where to go. In fact, he seems to run as much of his life like that as he can. Big Bob is not used to any kind of pushback or not getting his way. And much of the time, he relies on the threat of weapons to help him make his points. He brought guns on the trip, which ends up being a good thing for the family to try to protect themselves. His attitude about guns is tiresome to his family. He says to his wife, "I'd take my bullets over your prayers any day," and he mocks his son-in-law for not being comfortable with guns. In the end, Bob is dead, but the son-in-law saves the day with guns, so if the cop couldn't be the hero, at least the gun could be. This is similar to what we saw in *Dawn of the Dead* (2004). Bob's idea of masculinity is also imposed on the family. When he goes to look for help, early in the film, he leaves his young son in charge, instead of his wife or older daughter (or not appointing anyone to be in charge, for that matter, and trusting the adults to handle things). The word "pussy" is thrown around without regard for the female family members, and the men are in charge by default, driving the action.

This film is extremely pro-America, which was not uncommon for films of this era after 9/11. The American government is presented as morally correct, even though their nuclear testing made the hill people the way that they are. America is not seen as the enemy, because they tried to warn the locals, and because the locals chose to stay rather than be displaced, they apparently deserved their consequences. Being impacted by radiation changes their bodies and brains greatly, and the hill people become 'othered'. Bob has an American flag on his truck, which is shoved into his dead skull, perhaps meant to disgust the audience by desecrating a flag, which adds to the 'othering' of the hill people. Serving your country, listening to the authorities, and a hearty dose of gun ownership are presented positively in this film.

As the final film dissected in this book, perhaps it's appropriate that this film is one of the nastiest in terms of on-screen brutality. This film contains killing (of course), rape, animal death, a baby in peril, cannibalism, and acknowledgment of nuclear war. That's quite a bit for one horror remake to tackle. The two family dogs, German Shepherds named Beauty and Beast, have my sympathy. They seem well-loved, but their owners are careless, and they escape into the desert several times. A leash could solve that problem, but the family doesn't bother. Beauty is killed and gutted by the cannibals, and Beast finds her, a catalyst for his own revenge mission. (Even with the dogs, the male has to be in charge of the action.) Baby Catherine survives the film after she is rescued by her dad, but the cannibals called her "juicy" and evidently planned to eat her. The film doesn't go all the way to baby cannibalism, but the threat is present.

One of the most memorable scenes from the film is when Brenda (Emilie de Ravin) is raped. There is a scene that plays out like a suspenseful and tense home invasion in the camper trailer when the hill people attack the family. The cannibals, who earlier have captured and killed Bob, create a distraction by setting Bob's corpse ablaze on a makeshift pyre. Bobby (Dan Byrd), his mother (Kathleen Quinlan), and Doug (Aaron Stanford) come rushing out of the camper, and try to put the fire out, but it's too late. Beast is lured away by a man barking like a dog. The family is shocked, scared, and separated. This is when Brenda is attacked by two of the cannibal family and raped. It's a powerfully violent scene, with her trying to squirm away and make herself small, with nowhere to run in the tiny trailer. She is bleeding and crying, and the cannibals are saying horrible things to her. After she is raped and the cannibals have left, she's sitting alone on the bed where she was just attacked, wrapping herself in blankets, shaking and crying. No one in her family checks on her. She's all alone after what happened. It's harrowing.

The rest of the action in the trailer invasion scene is equally disturbing. A pet bird has its head bitten off and the hill person slurps up the blood. The mom is shot in the stomach before she can fight back. One of the cannibals points a gun at Baby Catherine (Maisie Camilleri Preziosi) while he gropes her mother, Lynne. They shoot Lynne before they leave, and Bobby, Brenda, and Doug are the only ones left. Bobby and Brenda have lost both their parents and their sister, and Doug has lost his wife. Beast has run off into the night.

The last act of the film is the surviving family members, plus Beast, who returns, trying to survive and rescue Catherine. Brenda is crying a lot, while Bobby is angry, each leaning into their gender roles for reacting to tragedy. Doug leads the final fights with the cannibal family and kills them. He walks triumphantly out of the hills with Beast and his baby and hugs his siblings-in-law. The film ends on a cliffhanger, with someone watching them through binoculars. There is a sequel, and it's less of a remake of the sequel to the original, and more of a sequel to Aja's film. It focuses on military personnel in the desert and doesn't offer any new information on the surviving family from the first film.

*The Hills Have Eyes* from 2006 leaves the viewer with a feeling that nothing is safe, no one is safe, and you need guns to protect your family. If you experience tragedy, you have to fight your way out of it and save yourself. It's a very American feeling, especially for the time period.

You're not from around here, are you?

As long as people have reason to fear one another, there will be horror stories about fear of The Other. While the anxieties of the

'70s have changes and been replaced with new troubles, there will always be room for stories about entitled middle-Americans and city folk wandering into places they haven't been invited. And those will always have the potential to be some of the scariest stories possible.

# CONCLUSION

## THE END OF AN ERA... BUT NOT THE END OF NASTY.

Millennial Nasties are a compelling collection of films. Each film is unique enough to warrant its own exploration in this book, but similar enough to other books to be part of a chapter, and similar enough to many others to be in this book. Across so many of the films, you can find horrible families, fear of The Other, fear of our systems failing us, and a warning that we need to protect ourselves. Some of this surely comes out of societal impacts of the time, such as 9/11, a looming recession, and presidential elections, to name a few. But some of it came from a desire to give audiences more of what they wanted, and what could be done creatively with the use of DVD players in many homes.

As I type this sentence in 2023, remakes are having another moment in horror, especially reboot/re-quel types of remakes. The *Scream* franchise is up to six films, with more in the works, and the tenth *Saw* film comes out soon. Horror fans will always want to return to our favorite stories, whether that's through remakes or sequels, but we love discovering new stories, too. The darkness in horror of recent years is more related to exploration of grief, mental illness, and trauma. Ideas of intersecting identities are explored, and representation of diversity is better, the Internet is inescapable in horror movies now, and there is an entire subgenre dedicated to social media influencers. While we still see bleak, heartbreaking films like *Hereditary* (Dir. Ari Aster, 2018), and violent, gory films like *Terrifier 2* (Dir. Damien Leone, 2022) and *Evil Dead Rise* (Dir. Lee Cronin, 2023), the era of torture porn is behind us.

And even though it's a subgenre I love, that's ok. Horror films are always reacting to the world around them, and it's a different world now. The horrors of our current world may be similar to previous generations' fears–for example, the war on Ukraine and the COVID-19 pandemic. War and sickness have always been explored through horror. But we have brand-new fears to explore as well, like the reality of sci-fi stories coming to life, as artificial intelligence is quickly getting scarier every day. We have abandoned some of the bigoted horror tropes, and there is room for many new voices in horror. More is possible now in indie filmmaking, and there are more ways to get creative than ever before. I will always love my Millennial Nasties, but I am excited about the future of horror.

There will never be another era like the Millennial Nasty era.

# SIX DEGREES OF SAW-PERATION

The following chart demonstrates how all of these films are connected, and they all connect back to the *Saw* franchise in six degrees or fewer.

- **1.** The *Saw* franchise connects to *The Strangers* through Kevin Greutert

- **1.** The *Saw* franchise connects to *Sorority Row* through Josh Stolberg

- **1.** The *Saw* franchise connects to the *Final Destination* franchise through Chad Donella and Gina Holden

- **1.** The *Saw* franchise connects to *Repo! The Genetic Opera*, the *Wrong Turn* franchise and the *Joy Ride* franchise through Dean Armstrong
- **2.** The *Wrong Turn* franchise connects to *Dawn of the Dead* through Kevin Zegers

- **1.** The *Saw* franchise connects to *The Last House on the Left* through Monica Potter
- **2.** *The Last House on the Left* connects to *The Hills Have Eyes* through Wes Craven
- **3.** *The Hills Have Eyes* connects to the *Joy Ride* franchise through Ted Levine
- **3.** *The Hills Have Eyes* connects to *P2* through Alexandre Aja

- **1.** The *Saw* franchise connects to *The Collector* through Marcus Dunstan
- **2.** *The Collector* connects to the *Hatchet* franchise through BJ McDonnell
- **3.** The *Hatchet* franchise connects to *Halloween/2* through Danielle Harris and Adam Weisman
- **3.** The *Hatchet* franchise connects to the *Final Destination* franchise through Tony Todd
- **4.** The *Final Destination* franchise connects to *Black Christmas* through Mary Elizabeth Winstead, Kristen Cloke, and Yan-Kay Crystal Lowe
- **5.** *Black Christmas* connects to the *Wrong Turn* franchise through Yan-Kay Crystal Lowe
- **6.** The *Wrong Turn* franchise connects to *Turistas* through Michael Arlen Ross
- **6.** The *Wrong Turn* franchise connects to *The Texas Chainsaw Massacre* through Erica Leerhsen
- **Bonus:** The *Wrong Turn* franchise connects back to the *Final Destination* franchise though Texas Battle

- The *Saw* franchise connects to Lionsgate as a part of the company's film library
- **1.** Lionsgate released *Repo! The Genetic Opera*
- **Bonus**: *Repo! The Genetic Opera* connects back to *Saw* through Darren Lynn Bousman

- **Bonus**: *Repo! The Genetic Opera* connects back to *House of 1000 Corpses/The Devil's Rejects* through Bill Moseley.

- **1.** Lionsgate released the *Hostel* franchise

- **1.** Lionsgate released *Cabin Fever*

- **1.** Lionsgate released *May*
- **Bonus:** *May* connects back to the *Wrong Turn* franchise through Jeremy Sisto

- **1.** Lionsgate released *Captivity*
- **2.** Connects to *House of Wax* through Elisha Cuthbert
- **3.** *House of Wax* connects to *Wolf Creek* and *The Loved Ones* because they were all filmed in Australia

- **1.** Lionsgate released *House of 1000 Corpses/The Devil's Rejects*
- **2.** *House of 1000 Corpses/The Devil's Rejects* connect to *Halloween/2* through Rob Zombie
- **3.** *Halloween/2* connect to *Dawn of the Dead* through Ken Foree
- **Bonus**: *Halloween/2* connect back to *Hatchet* through Danielle Harris and Adam Weisman

# THE **6** DEGREES OF

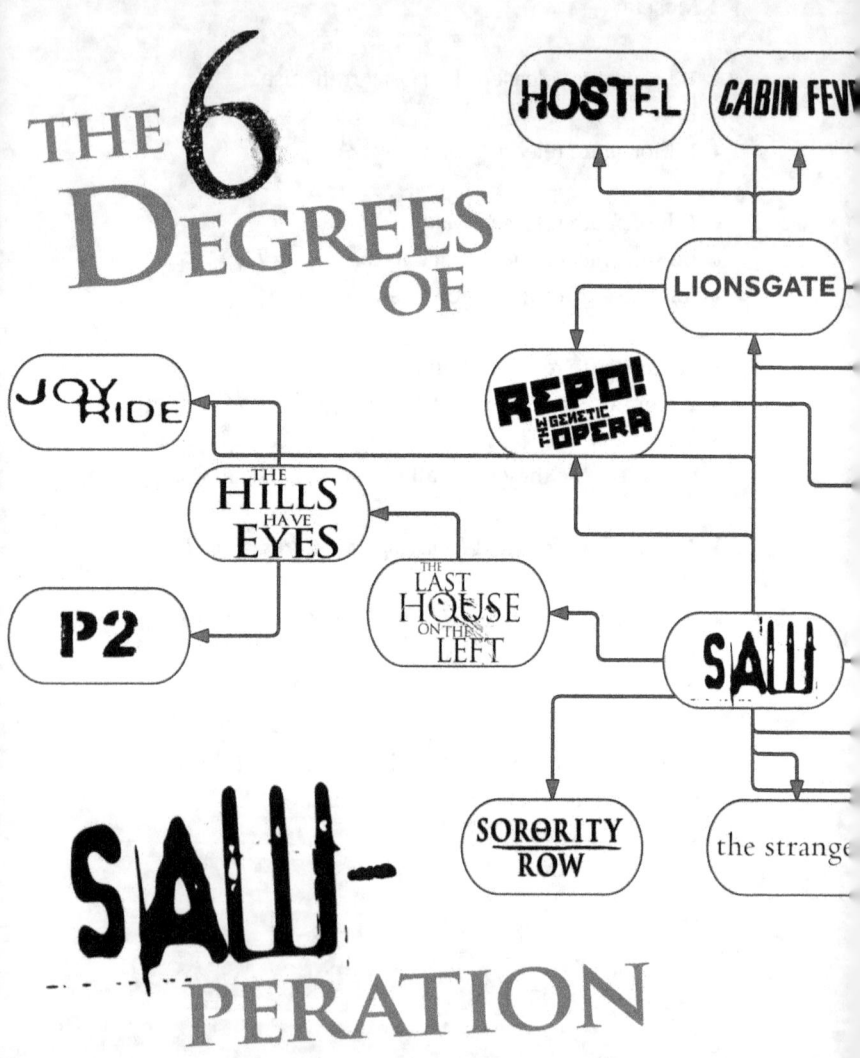

HOSTEL

CABIN FEVER

LIONSGATE

JOY RIDE

REPO! THE GENETIC OPERA

THE HILLS HAVE EYES

THE LAST HOUSE ON THE LEFT

P2

SAW

SORORITY ROW

the strange

# SAW-PERATION

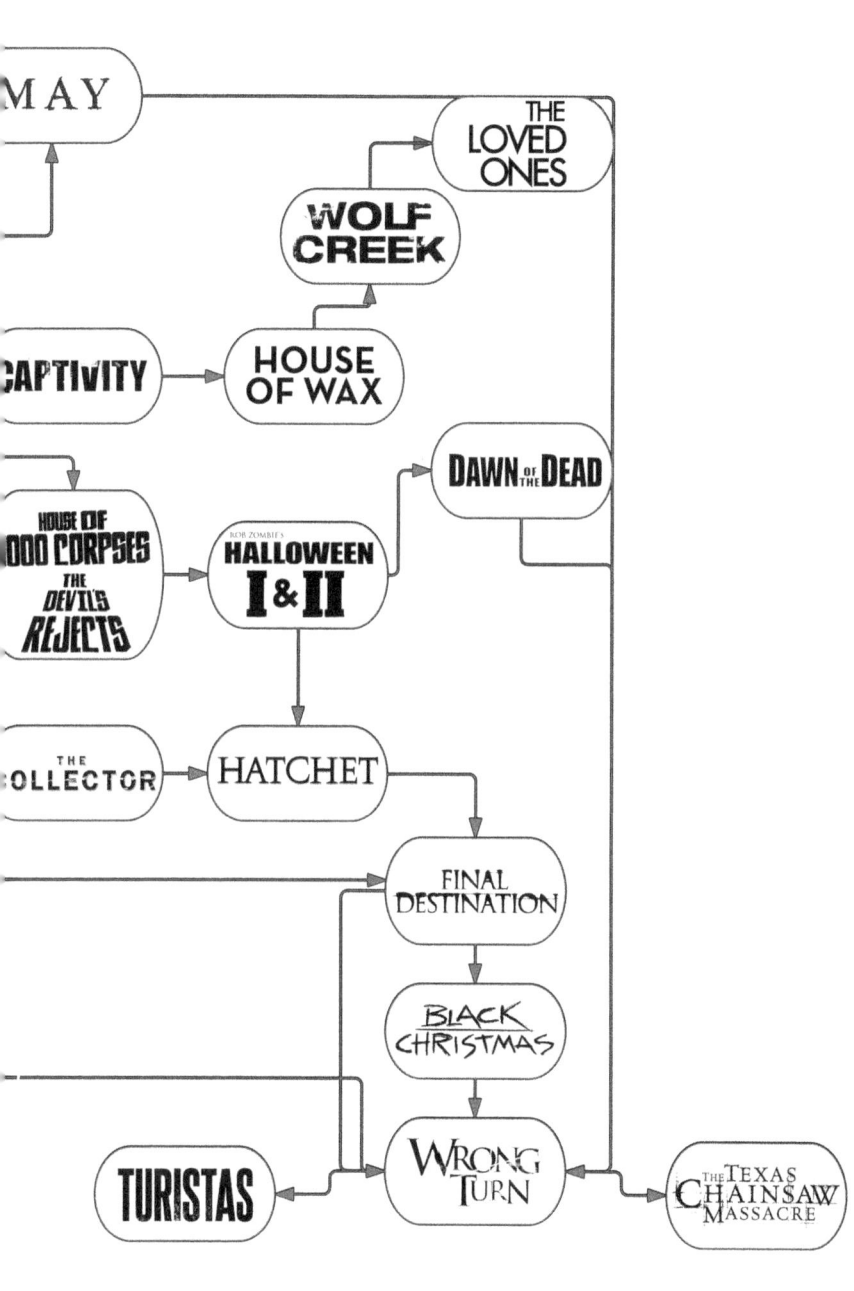

MAY

THE LOVED ONES

WOLF CREEK

CAPTIVITY → HOUSE OF WAX

DAWN OF THE DEAD

HOUSE OF 1000 CORPSES / THE DEVILS REJECTS → BOB ZOMBIE's HALLOWEEN I & II

THE COLLECTOR → HATCHET

FINAL DESTINATION

BLACK CHRISTMAS

TURISTAS ← WRONG TURN → THE TEXAS CHAINSAW MASSACRE

# REFERENCES

BBC News (2006, February 27). *Slovakia angered by horror film.* BBC News. http://news.bbc.co.uk/2/hi/entertainment/4754744.stm

Cinema.com. *Cabin Fever : Q & A With Writer/Director Eli Roth.* https://www.cinema.com/articles/2568/cabin-fever-q-a-with-writerdirector-eli-roth.phtml

Collis, Clark (2010, October 1). *'Hatchet II' director Adam Green slams the MPAA: 'They're evil.'* Entertainment Weekly. https://ew.com/article/2010/10/01/hatchet-2-unrated-mpaa-adam-green/

Condit, Jon (2006, January 2). *Roth, Eli (Hostel).* Dread Central. https://www.dreadcentral.com/news/3349/roth-eli-hostel/

Devine, Christian (date unknown). *American Nightmares: An Interview with Rob Zombie.* Christian Devine. http://www.christiandivine.com/RobZombie.htm

Edelstein, David (2006, February 6). *Now Playing at Your Local Multiplex: Torture Porn.* New York Magazine. https://web.archive.org/web/20071011200524/http:/nymag.com/movies/features/15622/

Hersh, Seymour (2004, April 30). *Torture at Abu Ghraib.* New Yorker. https://www.newyorker.com/magazine/2004/05/10/torture-at-abu-ghraib

Kennedy, Michael (2020, June 21). *Why Hatchet 2 Recast Marybeth Dunston With Danielle Harris.* Screen Rant. https://screenrant.com/hatchet-2-movie-marybeth-dunston-recast-danielle-harris/#why-hatchet-2-recast-marybeth-dunston-with-danielle-harris

Langberg, Eric (2020, June 25). *[Pride 2020] Outside Of Laramie: Joy Ride (2001) As Gay Panic Horror.* Gayly Dreadful. https://www.gaylydreadful.com/blog/pride-2020-outside-of-laramie-joy-ride-2001-as-gay-panic-horror

Miska, Brad (2009, July 13). *How 'The Collector' Was Almost a Prequel to Saw!* Bloody Disgusting. https://bloody-disgusting.com/news/16731/

Powers-Schaub, Ariel (2021, July 15). *Hostel (2005).* Ghouls Magazine. https://www.ghoulsmagazine.com/articles/hostel-2005-review

Powers-Schaub, Ariel (2021 July 19). *House of 1000 Corpses (2003).* Ghouls Magazine. https://www.ghoulsmagazine.com/articles/house-1000-corpses-film-review

Powers-Schaub, Ariel (2021, September 28). *"I've never killed anyone": The Hypocrisy of Jigsaw.* Ghouls Magazine. https://www.ghoulsmagazine.com/articles/the-hypocrisy-of-jigsaw-in-saw-movies

Universal Pictures (2009, April 19). *The Strangers Production Notes.* Hollywood Jesus. https://web.archive.org/web/20121030105847/http:/hollywoodjesus.com/movies/strangers/notes.pdf

Wixson, Heather (2010, February 11). *Eli Roth Talks Cabin Fever, Hostel 3, Endangered Species, Thanksgiving, and More!* Dread Central. https://web.

# References

archive.org/web/20131228130559/http://www.dreadcentral.com/news/
35838/eli-roth-talks-cabin-fever-hostel-3-endangered-species-thanksgiving-
and-more

# ACKNOWLEDGMENTS

I have been lucky to have so much help and support; it feels almost impossible to thank everyone enough.

Big "thank you" to Ghouls Magazine. They took a chance on me when I had no writing experience and just wanted to pitch my ideas analyzing the *Saw* franchise. It gave me a place to hone my skills and realize that people wanted to read what I had to say. This book would, quite literally, not exist without Ghouls. If you are a Ghoul, I love you, and I know you have cheered me on, and I thank you for that. Thanks especially to Zoë Rose Smith and Rebecca McCallum, the EIC and the Assistant Editor, who make me a better writer.

Thank you to Encyclopocalypse publications. Much like Ghouls Magazine, they took a chance on a new writer, and changed my life. My birthdays have been cursed, and I always try to avoid acknowledging my birthday, lest something bad happen. But the Encyclopocalypse team said "yes" to me on my birthday, out of pure coincidence, and so I guess the curse is lifted. Thank you also to my editor, Candace Nola.

Thank you to Lex Cashore. When I was first telling my friends about my idea for a book, I would say, "I'm writing this book that no one asked for" in a self-deprecating way. One day, Lex said, "Hey Ariel, will you please write this book?" So, someone had actually asked for it and I had to stop saying that. That was a thoughtful move on Lex's part.

Everyone who read some part or all of this book while it was in progress and gave me feedback: Nicole Steck, Caleb Durward, Iona Smith, Bel Morrigan, Mike Snoonian, and my mom, Gail Powers-Schaub. Everyone who offered to read also gets a "thank you," there were just so many offers. Thank you to Janine Pipe for the advice all the way through the process, and her unwavering support.

Every single one of my friends and family who would occasionally ask, "How's the book going?" Knowing you cared about my project made me feel validated, so thank you. Especially those of you who hate horror movies. Thanks for caring about me, anyway.

Anyone who has ever hosted me on a podcast or published my writing, thank you for giving me more space to share my ideas.

And to my husband, who enthusiastically supported me the entire time, even though he hates these films, and we were also doing a DIY basement renovation at the same time. He did a lot of work himself so I could work on my book. Love you.

# ABOUT THE AUTHOR

Ariel Powers-Schaub is a horror film critic and analyst from the midwestern United States. She is a writer and a podcaster who champions 2000s horror. Her first horror memory is being terrified, but fascinated, by Hexxus, the pollution monster in *FernGully* (1992), and she has been chasing that feeling ever since. She is obsessed with Halloween and probably planning this year's party as we speak. Find her across social media platforms at @Ari_Hellraiser.

# Index